BUILDING A
MOBILE APP

A RESOURCE GUIDE FOR CLIENTS & CORPORTATIONS

Building a Mobile App: A Resource Guide for Clients and Corporations

www.ambersawaya.com
www.buildingamobileapp.com

Cover art and interior layout collaboration by Kira Griffin.
Proofing and editing by Karen Kaminski.
Marketing by Hendrix Marketing Results, LLC.

First Edition: October 2012
Second Edition: May 2013

Printed in the United States of America.

ISBN-13: 978-1480060869
ISBN-10: 1480060860

BUILDING A
MOBILE APP

A RESOURCE GUIDE FOR CLIENTS & CORPORTATIONS

[SECOND EDITION]

by Amber Sawaya

www.buildingamobileapp.com

REVIEWS FOR BUILDING A MOBILE APP

UNFAMILIAR TOPIC BECAME UNDERSTANDABLE

"The author uses humor, clarity, brevity and simple bullet points to render this topic user friendly. Most of us are not going to build a mobile app today, but if you wanted to explore the topic this book is a must. You will know enough to get you into the game and have an informed conversation. The examples are a valuable learning experience to pull everything together."

—Amazon Reviewer, Colorado Author

A PARTICULARLY GOOD INVESTMENT. IT'S ALL GRAIN, NO CHAFF.

"I bought this book for a social media infrastructure project I am pursuing, and it turns out to have been a particularly good investment. It's all grain, no chaff. It helped me educate myself on the basic issues involved in app-building, which forms part of my project."

—Amazon Reviewer, Nolivienne C. Ermitaño

THANK YOU! BUILDING A MOBILE APP HAS GIVEN ME THE CONFIDENCE TO TALK TO PROSPECTIVE DEVELOPERS.

"Just finished your book and wanted to say thank you. I have no prior experience in this field and your clear and simple (it had to be for me) to read book has given me the confidence to talk to prospective developers with at least a chance of understanding them."

—M. Delahaye, Six Fields UK

EVERYONE WILL LEARN FROM THIS BOOK

"As a life-long software engineer that has transitioned to mobile app development, my focus has typically been on design and implementation of any given project. This book gives me very good high-level insight into the challenges that many people have to go through before they ever talk to me about building their app. While I try to be aware of such things, Building a Mobile App was a fantastic reminder of the journey all of the other folks on any team striving to build an app go through.

While this is geared towards those folks that are considering an app for their needs, *anyone* involved in the process can learn from reading this book.

If you do app development, get this book, it's that simple."

—Amazon Reviewer, Everydave

GET YOUR FREE "MOBILE APP PLANNING BLUEPRINT"

The Mobile App Planning Blueprint will help you get the most leverage from your apps by getting you and your company off to the right start. This document will help with your initial planning—leaving you with a better, clearer plan for for completing your mobile app on time and on budget.

Register today for free access:
www.buildingamobileapp.com/blueprint

CREATE A BETTER APP BUILD EXPERIENCE

I wrote this book to answer your questions before you even knew what to ask. You are not alone—everybody who starts an app project has these questions.

You can connect with me on Facebook:
www.facebook.com/authorambersawaya

And on Google+: +AmberSawaya

CONTENTS

DEDICATION

This book is dedicated to our clients—a fantastic group of people that has allowed us to experiment, learn, and work with them to create great things

A NOTE OF CAUTION

This book is correct as of the publish date—but things in the mobile and responsive design world are moving quickly.

From here we'll see the number of apps in each store grow, Android and iOS continue to jockey for position and I have my fingers crossed that a decent shell or wrapper platform will grow up enough to be a viable way to cut development costs. There is always talk about who is in third position (will it be BlackBerry or Windows Phone or maybe someone else?).

There are always rumors of what is coming out next, but no real way to prepare for them.

GET STARTED /
GOOD THINGS TO KNOW

WHO THIS BOOK IS FOR

This book is for account managers, project managers, MarComm groups, CEOs, admins, accountants, and principals. It's for executive teams, planning committees, and people with big ideas.

In short—it's for everyone involved in building an app who won't be putting in the wrench time as a designer or developer.

This book will help you align your team, understand what goes into an app, and (maybe most importantly) help you speak to the designers and developers in a way everyone understands.

"Ah...designers and developers..."

Whether you read that heading fondly, with a touch of sarcasm, or you turn the "ah" into a scream—this book is here to help. How do you best communicate with the fancy glasses and ironic haircuts? How do you talk to their socks-and-sandals counterparts? How do you exit the interaction feeling like you are getting somewhere (and not feeling like you're not nearly cool enough to talk to the former and way too cool to talk to the latter)? We're going to need some common ground.

I've been a designer for more than a decade, in a variety of roles. I've been creative director in charge of in-house design teams, I've been a worker bee in agencies, and currently I run a successful design and IT firm with my partner. I am primarily responsible for finding and managing clients and projects, but still serve as creative director and often designer on app projects. My partner is a developer. It's this alignment of a designer and a developer working closely with clients that prompted this book.

If you have completed a design/development project before—maybe a website or a corporate tool—or you work with your internal designers and developers regularly, the following stories should strike a chord. If you haven't worked with these interesting folks, consider this your intro to what you can expect.

TALK NERDY TO ME

Design and Development Notes in the Book

Ok, so why am I telling you all this? Throughout this book you will see some fairly detailed information about the design and development inner workings. This isn't to turn you into a pixel pusher or a hacker. It's so that you can have informed conversations with your team.

Sections of the book that are helpful for everyone on the project but specifically speak to designers and developers will be formatted as shown below.

So let's get to it!

> **Especially for geeks.**
>
> Sections of the book that are helpful for everyone on the project but specifically speak to designers and developers are formatted like this.

PROPER CARE AND FEEDING OF DESIGNERS & DEVELOPERS

Just a quick note from someone who now gets to hand-pick clients: **Be good to your designers and developers.**

We understand we are very different. We are interested in strange things, we do all sorts of nerdy things for fun, we are strongly opinionated on things that can seem trivial.

Remember we are craftspeople. We take great care and pride in what we produce and for every hour of what you see produced, we spend dozens of hours in and out of work thinking about and coming up with that solution. Treat us like a partner and demand the same from us.

I've seen too many projects hit the "GTFO zone." (For those not familiar with the acronym, it's get the !@#$* out.) This is the zone where everyone on the team is so bedraggled that they want to do the bare minimum to get it done and get it out the door—this happens from the client, designer, and developer side. It doesn't have to be this way if everyone stays in it to win it and respects each others' feedback.

FIVE SHORT STORIES ABOUT WORKING WITH DESIGNERS & DEVELOPERS

#1: CHANGES

"Will you make this swipe instead of scroll?"

What sounds like a simple request often turns out not to be. All of a sudden your team seems flustered: "We can, but that will completely derail the launch date and is out of scope."

So what happened? How can a seemingly simple request cause that much backlash? Well, in this particular instance that part of the project is probably coded and locked in. Changing it requires throwing out and starting over on a hefty piece of functionality—that is why your developer is downing Mountain Dews and giving you the stink eye and your designer threw herself on the floor.

A scroll works differently than a swipe, requiring different cues to the user about how to use it, which means the design needs to be reworked to facilitate these cues. Adding a little more space here or there can throw off the whole grid the design is aligned to and cause a substantial redesign to accommodate the smallest of elements.

The moral of the story:
Anything regarding functionality needs to be discussed as early as possible. Arm yourself with knowledge of functional possibilities by downloading other well done apps and finding things you like. And frame your question as an

exploratory request. Something like, "Is it possible at this point to change this from scrolling to a swipe? What would be involved in that?"

#2 : MORE CHANGES

"Can you change all the links to red?"

Yep. Done, anything else?

The moral of the story:
Sometimes it really is that easy. Never be afraid to ask.

#3: VALID FEEDBACK

"My spouse/friend/child doesn't like this."

It's good to keep in mind that the feedback of people invested in the project and of end-users is important; however, one person's initial reaction to something isn't terribly useful if they don't understand the goals of a project, the scope, and factors such as time and budget.

It also depends on who this person is. If it's your boss and they have a vested interest in the project—yes, it needs to be addressed. If it's an important customer that will use the product, their feedback has some merit. If your kid doesn't understand how to use the mobile app we are building for your sales force...well, it's kind of tough luck on that one. The same is true if your mom doesn't like your logo — these people are not your target audience.

Similarly, you can have a bunch of invested parties give feedback and end up with a myriad of comments and requests. You need to filter these and make sure you aren't designing by committee, which can lead to watered-down design and functionality in which the only goal is to make everyone at the table agree.

The moral of the story:
Feedback that comes from someone who isn't invested in the project or part of your target audience isn't necessarily valid. Design by committee creates watered down work.

#4: TRUST YOUR TEAM

"Have you tried it in green or maybe thought about adding a picture of kittens and toasters?"

Trust your team. You didn't hire someone to be a pixel puppet, you hired someone with expertise to think about your project and provide a solution. Your designers and developers are doing much more than making something look good—they are solving a problem and ensuring the end-user has a great experience.

Trust that your team has thought this through. They've thought a lot about your project, done several of these for other clients, looked at lots of different options, and are only providing you with the best solutions.

The moral of the story:
Trust that your team has thought this through and is providing only the best solution to you.

#5: CLIENT RESPONSIBILITIES

"We'll get you content after we see the design."

Sometimes, this is totally possible, but think of it like building a house: Your architect can't design your house until she knows how big the house is, what kinds of things are important to you, and where the house will be. It's a waste of everyone's time because there is no way the original drawing will be what you want.

The moral of the story:
You are a partner in this project. From educating yourself on the project (thank goodness you bought this book!) to providing content in a timely fashion, you are as much a part of this project as the team you hire.

PART 1 /
WHY BUILD A MOBILE APP

WHY BUILD A MOBILE APP?

It could be because of a stray comment from the CEO: **"We should have an app!"**

It could be because you need a better way to share information with your sales force. It could be because you need a different—or better—way to reach your audience.

"When was the last time you saw a C-level executive, business manager, or someone in a market segment you are trying to reach without a mobile device?"[1]

Whatever the reason, you started with a vague notion of making an app. In July 2011 we were being asked to help clients turn their own vague notions into real projects. From our experiences then, we distilled four concepts for building an app:

- **Capsule Experience**
- **Point of Access**
- **Depth of Information**
- **Extended Capabilities**

A couple years and a handful of successful apps later, these concepts still hold.

---

1 Dye, John. "AdNews Online Only." Last modified May 29, 2011. Accessed June 1, 2011. http://www.adnewsonline.com/pub_article.cfm?artID=1309.

OUTSIDE
DISTRACTIONS

COMPLEX OR
EXTRANEOUS TOOLS

CAPSULE EXPERIENCE
A specific tool set in a simplified environment
which make specific tasks focused and easier.

CAPSULE EXPERIENCE

Apps are a great way to build a **capsule experience**—a completely controlled environment in which to pull together and deliver your information.

You may already have all the content you need for your app—it's just in blog posts, presentations, sales sheets, and other places. Pulling it into one branded experience is a great way to deliver it to existing and potential customers.

Putting this into one capsule also helps keep users focused on your content just a little longer than other places where noise and distractions are just a click away.

 **CASE STUDY**   **Example Case Study**
Capsule Experience: The Mandate Press / page 100

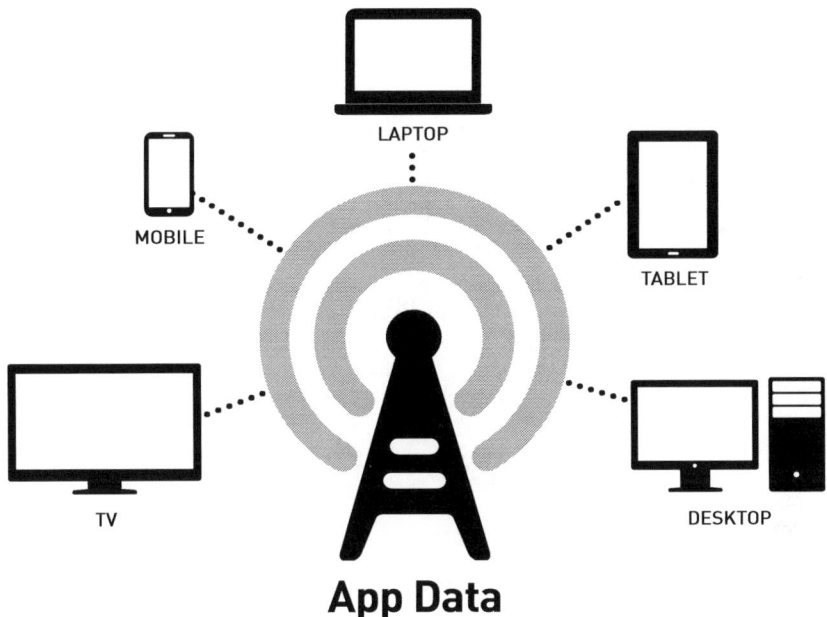

App Data

POINT OF ACCESS

This strategy takes a much broader view of an application. Instead of creating a controlled environment, this approach puts the information in the center and uses each device as a **point of access**. The presentation of information is modified for the user interface of each device. This keeps interactions with your information as efficient as possible.

Some examples of this in the marketplace are **Evernote**, **Reeder**, and **Things** (products we use and love). In this scenario, you could either refer to the product as "the Evernote App" or "Evernote, which can also be accessed via an iPhone app."

An example of a point of access app is the TimeMD app. It uses iPads and Android Tablets in place of costly time clocks—and adds extra functionality to boot.

CASE STUDY **Example Case Study**
Point of Access: TimeMD / page 102

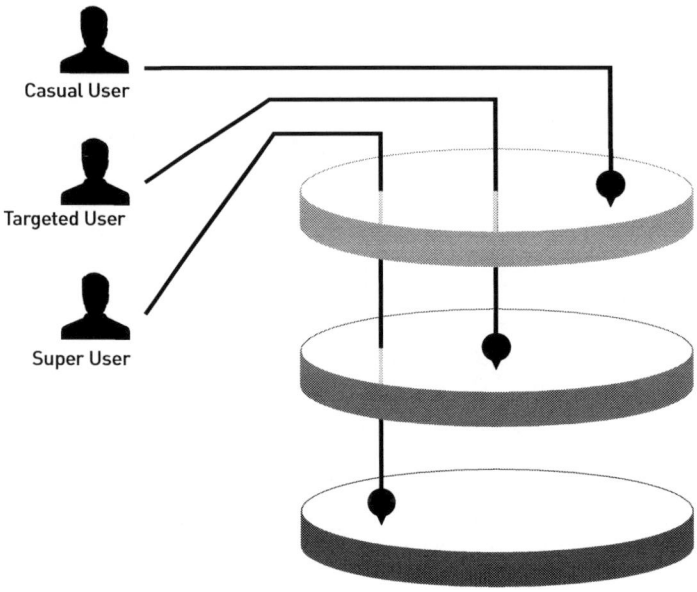

Casual User

Targeted User

Super User

FOUNDATION
The Casual User opens the app once or twice and tries it out, and is able to immediately understand the basics of how to use it.

COMPREHENSION
The Targeted User has gone through most of the apps screens and understands how to do the main tasks some what frequently.

APPLICATION
The Super User knows the app in and out, uses all its abilities regularly and would like new features added to increase its usefulness.

DEPTH OF INFORMATION

Depth of Information is looking at your content as several layers.

In a static document or book, there is essentially one plane that you read through from beginning to end. In an app, you can step a user through understanding one piece at a time.

You start by presenting simple concepts and functionality to your users. When they have the basic framework, you allow them to dive down a level, then another, and so on.

It's important to realize that some users only need the tip of the iceberg and your app should accommodate them, while others want to go past even your targeted use to mastery.

EXTENDED CAPABILITIES

One of the biggest reasons to move to an app is extended capabilities, or all the neat little widgets and gizmos that can be built into an app using native or custom code.

It's best to start with your concept then see what you can make that concept DO in between what it is saying. It's the marriage of information and function that makes an app great—information is useful once or twice, but a tool can be useful many times.

See the next page for a big list of extended capabilities ideas.

CASE STUDY

Example Case Study
Extended Capabilities: Boart Longyear / page 95

CASE STUDY

Example Case Study
Extended Capabilities: SmartMouth / page 98

Extended capabilities need to be customized per app, but here are a few suggestions:

» **Navigation** – the personal interaction with an app allows for different and interesting navigation schemes.

– **Table of contents** – simple navigation that people are used to.

– **Topical** – similar to website navigation, users choose which topic they want to visit.

– **Use case based** – we like to call this "choose your own adventure," i.e. navigation that changes based on who you are, your role, where you are, or other user-centered orders.

– **By task** – reading, task lists, goal lists, etc.

» **Search** – make sure users can find anything that's available in the app.

» **Rich media** – display audio and visual in an app.

» **Glossary** – don't lose your audience over a single word. Define terms and present them inline with a tap.

» **Forums** – build a place inside the app where people can discuss the information presented.

» **Task lists** – lists of things to do can be customized by the user and then checked off in the app or emailed for use externally.

» **Quizzes** – a good way to know if the information is being interpreted as intended, for both the user and creator.

» **Bookmark** – mark particular screens that are useful.

» **Highlight** – highlight certain parts of text for your own

SPECIALIZED SEARCH

ECOMMERCE

TASK LISTS

USER CREATED CONTENT

CONTACT GROUPS

reference or to share via email or social media.

» **Notes** – leave notes in context with a way to search through those notes.

» **User created media** – pictures, audio, and video that can be submitted back through the app.

» **Advertisements** – sell ad space to monetize an app.

» **Internal advertisements** – set up dedicated space (as for advertisements) but then use it for internal content, such as the launch of a new product or a reminder to submit TPS reports. This information can be triggered (the TPS reports only remind people on the last four work days of the month) or pushed (new product launch).

» **Updates** – send out new content as it is finished, fix mistakes, or refresh images (a corporate

directory that refreshes when new photos are taken, for example).

» **Internal browser** – keep people in the app if any function requires them to go online.

» **Attribution** – link to the author of particular content, complete with a page about them and a way to contact them from the app.

» **Acronym lookup** – have you ever read something with so many acronyms that it's like reading a bowl of alphabet soup? Put in an acronym lookup. Or take an even more sophisticated approach: Make the acronym expandable with a tap and then link all the usages of that acronym, so that once someone knows what it stands for they can click the word again and the entire app updates to only show the acronym.

» **FAQs** – open and close information that people need to know or even allow users to submit questions

AUGMENTED REALITY

FORUMS

TASK SPECIFIC TOOLS

FINANCE

REPORTING

in an app or about specific text sections.

» **Maps/geolocation** – show users where something is in relation to where they are.

» **Augmented reality** – overlay data on the real world. Examples include using the device's camera to look at a street and have the restaurants and ATMs show up as graphical overlays.

» **Annual catalog app** – You scan a catalog page with your mobile device and the inside of closets are revealed or a 3D bed appears to sit on the page in front of you. This was done in the IKEA 2013 catalog.

» **Cataloging/reporting** – allow users to report damages or catalog things they see that you want to know about.

» **Translation/localization** – deliver your app in several languages, or go one step further and update language, currency, images, contact info, etc. Either let your users choose which language to view, or serve it to them based on location.

» **eCommerce** - allow shopping and ordering from the app (also called mCommerce for mobile commerce).

» **Toolsets for users** – you could create very simple micro-apps in your app to extend the extended capabilities (see what we did there?).

  – **For copywriters** you could include a dictionary, thesaurus, or language manuals.

  – **Chefs** could have measurement conversions, quick substitutions, or guides to local fresh ingredients.

  – **Designers** could have PMS colors, client contracts, views into project management systems, etc.

The more defined and specific the user base is, the deeper you can make the toolsets in the app.

WHAT COULD BE A GOOD MOBILE APP FOR YOUR COMPANY?

Depending on who is leading the creating of a mobile app at your company, you may be looking for a specific idea. If you haven't been tasked with specifically solving a business problem and instead you have a vague request to "get us a mobile app," here are some ideas to get started:

- Take public information that is useful for your customers and brand it for your company.

- Make an event app. Include videos of keynote speeches, trade show floor maps, check-in systems, sponsor pages, etc.

- Distribute your company's business goals as an app to all employees.

- Put out your next catalog as an app. You can include background information on products, videos of usage, and online ordering from the app.

- Take a complex concept in your organization and present it differently to each department so they can better understand it from their point of view.

- Make a campus app with maps to buildings, lists of business functions, scheduling information, and an employee directory.

IS THERE MONEY IN APPS?

Oh yes. There is. For you, your company, designers, developers, device makers, and app stores.

As soon as Apple opened the flood gates and allowed developers to create apps people started calling it "the app gold rush". Soon Google threw open the doors and let people start building open-source apps. So where are we now?

In my opinion the app gold rush is just about over—but only for people that put out crappy little apps for 99¢ and end up making a fortune. There is too much competition and users have "app fatigue"—too many apps in general and too many that don't deliver.

We are, however, still in the first inning of apps. Really good games, incredibly well thought out informational pieces, and highly functional tools are just barely coming to life. Large corporations are seeing new ways to connect with customers and deliver value and the expected growth is exponential.

Apps are important to our economy as well, in 2012 we saw the increase in brand awareness in mobile with Apple snagging the #2 Best Global Brand spot (up 129%, #1 was Coca-Cola), Amazon up 46%, and Samsung up 40%.[1]

---

1 Sweet, Laura. "If It's Hip, It's Here: The Top 100 Global Brands of 2012. Who's Moving Up, Who's Dominating and Who's Declining." If It's Hip, It's Here. Accessed April 22, 2013. http://ifitshipitshere.blogspot.com/2012/10/the-top-100-global-brands-of-2012-whos.html.

1 Reisinger, Don. "Mobile app revenue set to soar to $46 billion in 2016 | The Digital Home - CNET News." Technology News - CNET News. Last modified February 16, 2012. Accessed September 10, 2012. http://news.cnet.com/8301-13506_3-57379364-17/mobile-app-revenue-set-to-soar-to-$46-billion-in-2016/.

$9 Billion:
Made on apps in 2012[1]

$46 Billion:
Forecasted app revenue by 2016[2]

WHO HAS A MOBILE DEVICE?

First off, let's clarify what a mobile device is. When I originally presented this information in 2010 all we were concerned about was smartphones. Now we consider a larger juggernaut of mobile devices, including phones and tablets.

Almost 75 percent of the US population has a mobile device. When we first put together this report to share with clients that number was 25 percent—and that was only a few years ago.

1 ComScore, and MobiLens. "comScore Reports May 2012 U.S. Mobile Subscriber Market Share - comScore. Inc." comScore, Inc. - Measuring the Digital World. Last modified July 2, 2012. Accessed September 1, 2012. http://www.comscore.com/Press_Events/Press_Releases/2012/7/comScore_Reports_May_2012_U.S._Mobile_ Subscriber_Market_Share.

2 "U.S. & World Population Clocks." Census Bureau Homepage. Accessed September 29, 2012. http://www. census.gov/main/www/popclock.html.

* If devices were distributed evenly among the population—however it is more likely that a smaller percentage of people have multiple devices (i.e. an iPhone and an iPad).

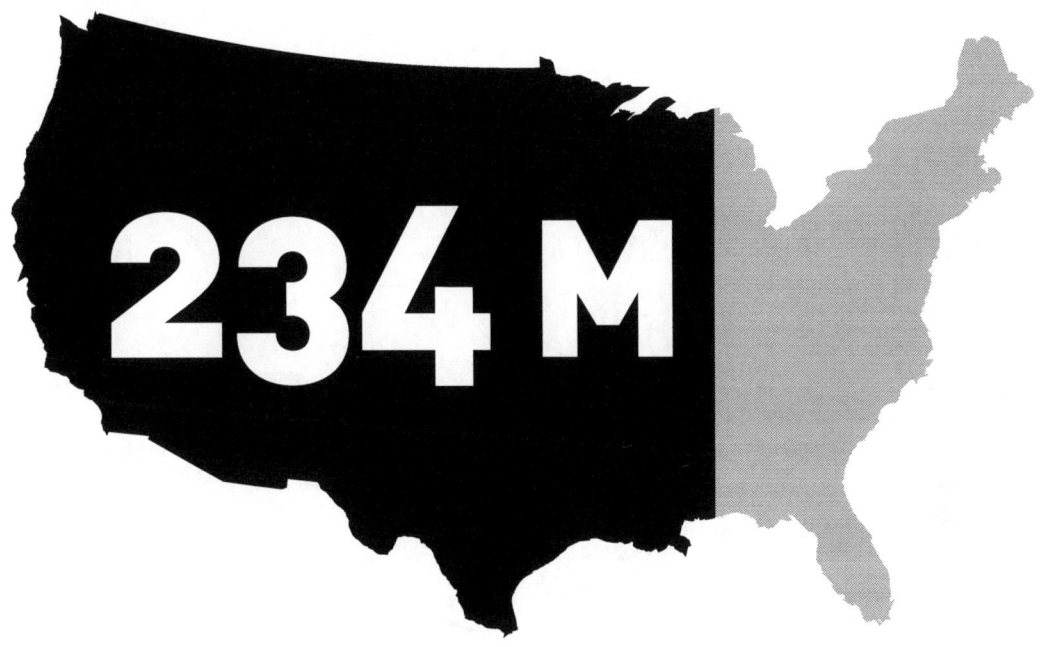

234 million Americans have mobile devices[1]
(smartphones & tablets)

—————————— *which equals** ——————————

3 in 4 people in the U.S.[2]

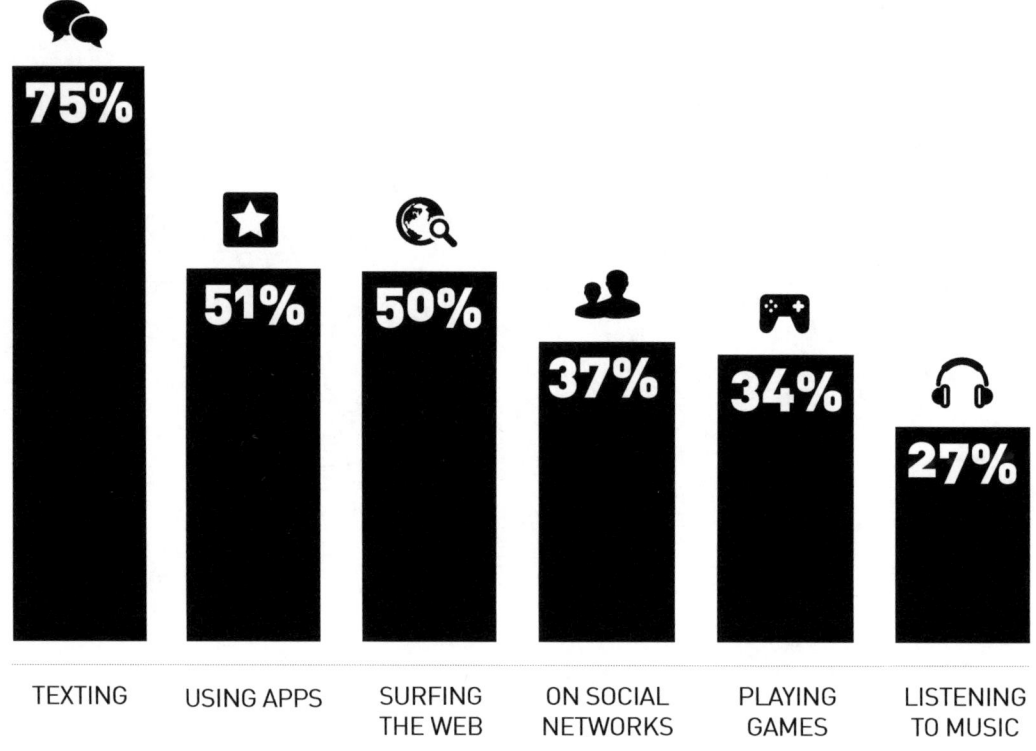

TEXTING	USING APPS	SURFING THE WEB	ON SOCIAL NETWORKS	PLAYING GAMES	LISTENING TO MUSIC
75%	51%	50%	37%	34%	27%

WHAT ARE PEOPLE DOING WITH THESE DEVICES?

Yes, these are phones, but people aren't using them to call Mom. They are texting, using apps, surfing the web, using social media, gaming, and listening to music.[1]

1 **Mobile Content Usage**
   3 month average ending May 2012 vs 3 month average ending February 2012.
   Total U.S. Smartphone Subscribers (Smartphones & Non-Smartphone) Ages 13+

   ComScore, and MobiLens. "comScore Reports May 2012 U.S. Mobile Subscriber Market Share - comScore, Inc." comScore, Inc. - Measuring the Digital World. Last modified July 2, 2012. Accessed September 29, 2012. http://www.comscore.com/Press_Events/Press_Releases/2012/7/comScore_Reports_May_2012_U.S._Mobile_Subscriber_Market_Share.

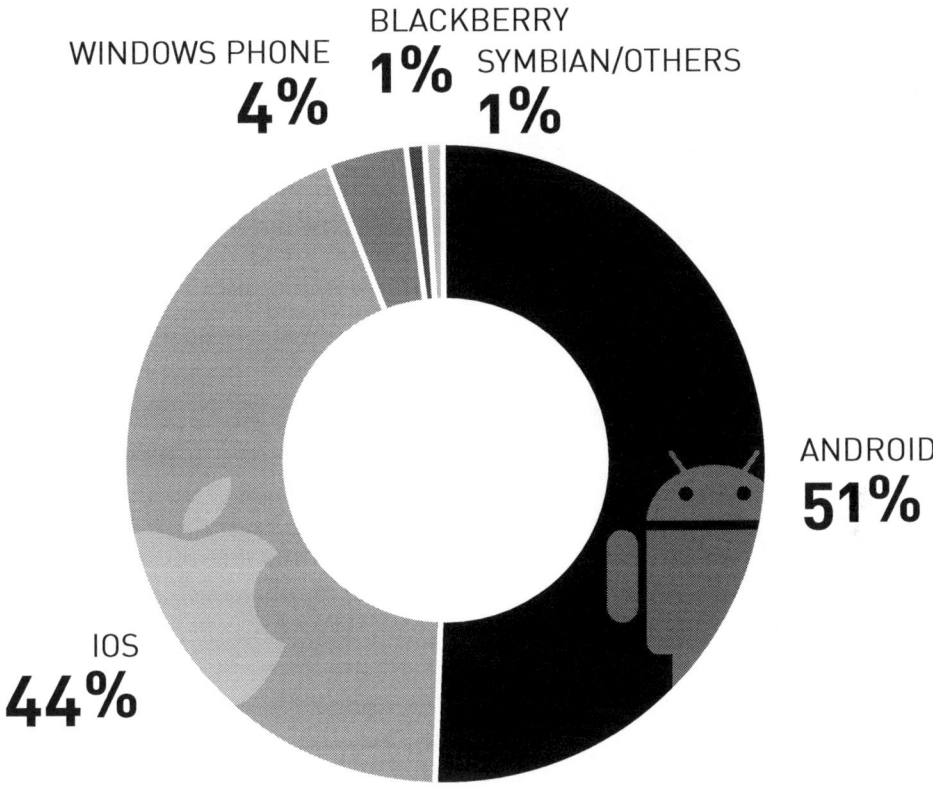

WINDOWS PHONE
4%

BLACKBERRY
1%

SYMBIAN/OTHERS
1%

ANDROID
51%

IOS
44%

WHICH PLATFORM DO THEY USE?

Mostly iOS and Android, with some BlackBerry, Windows Phone, and Symbian being reported. When this book was originally published BlackBerry held 11% market share. In the course of a year (Feb 2012–2013) they lost 81% of their share while Windows Phone gained 52% and was able to snag the number three spot on the graph.[1]

1 Koetsier, John. "Android up 13%, iOS down 7%, BlackBerry down 81% ... and Windows Phone up a massive 52%." VentureBeat. Accessed April 22, 2013. http://venturebeat.com/2013/04/01/android-up-13-ios-down-7-blackberry-down-81-and-windows-phone-up-a-massive-52/.

WHO HAS WHAT[1]?: ANDROID

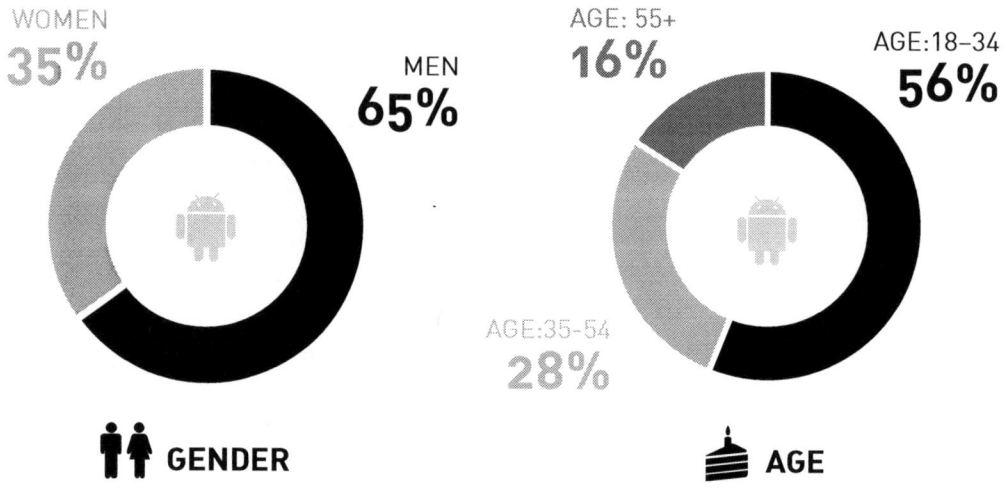

WOMEN
35%

MEN
65%

GENDER

AGE: 55+
16%

AGE:18–34
56%

AGE:35-54
28%

AGE

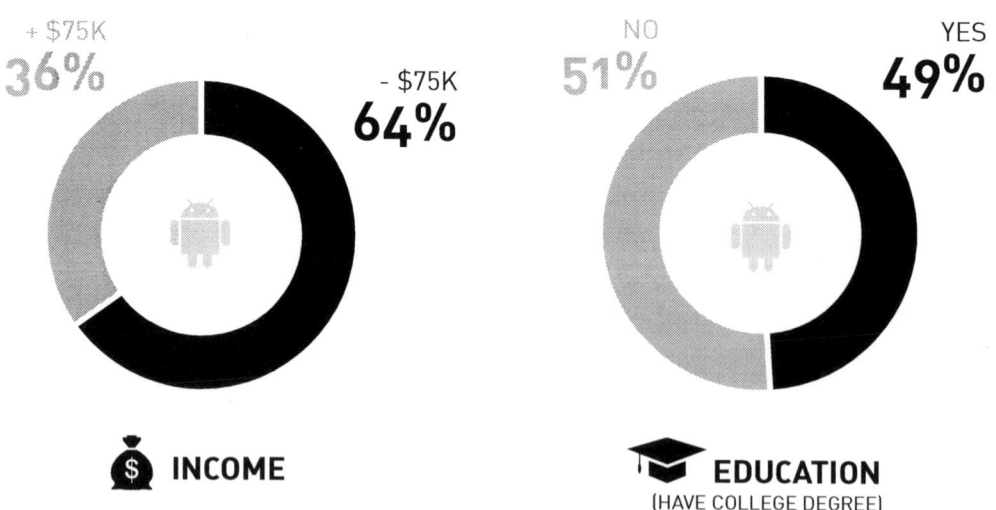

+ $75K
36%

- $75K
64%

INCOME

NO
51%

YES
49%

EDUCATION
(HAVE COLLEGE DEGREE)

1 Racoma, J. Angelo. "iPhone users older, richer, better-educated." Android Authority | Android News - Phones - Tablets - Apps - Reviews. Last modified August 2, 2012. Accessed August 22, 2012. http://www. androidauthority.com/are-iphone-users-richer-better-educated-than-android-users-105032.

WHO HAS WHAT?: IPHONE

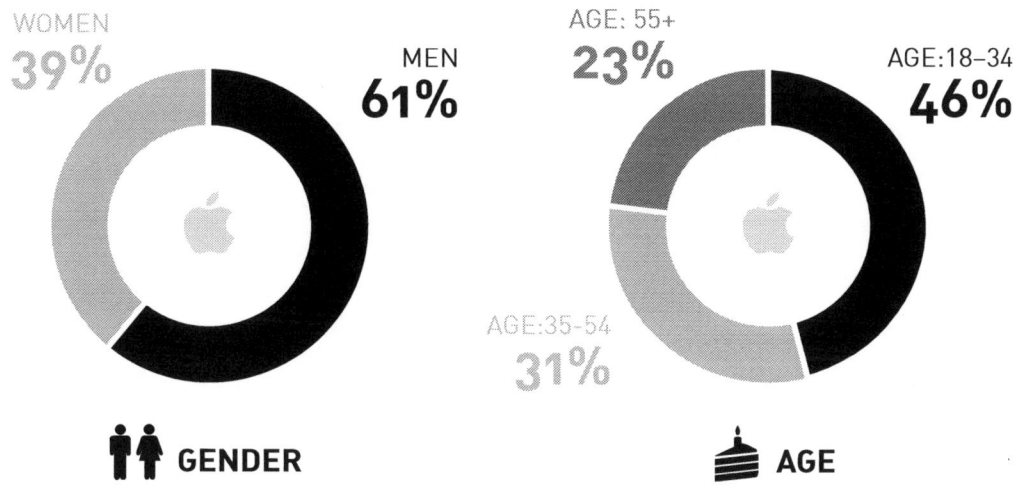

WOMEN
39%

MEN
61%

AGE: 55+
23%

AGE:18–34
46%

AGE:35-54
31%

GENDER

AGE

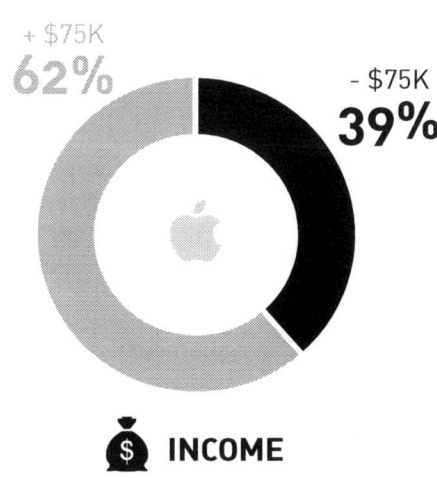

+ $75K
62%

- $75K
39%

INCOME

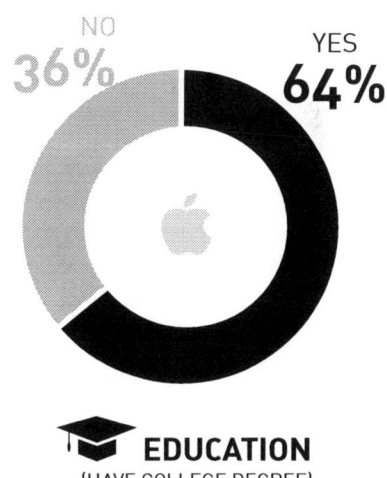

NO
36%

YES
64%

EDUCATION
(HAVE COLLEGE DEGREE)

WHO HAS WHAT?: BLACKBERRY

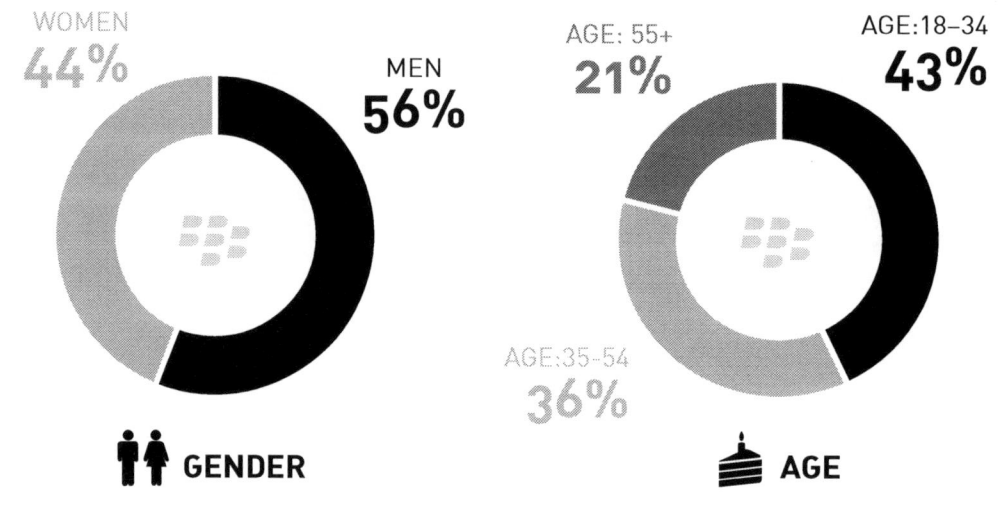

WOMEN
44%

MEN
56%

GENDER

AGE: 55+
21%

AGE:18–34
43%

AGE:35-54
36%

AGE

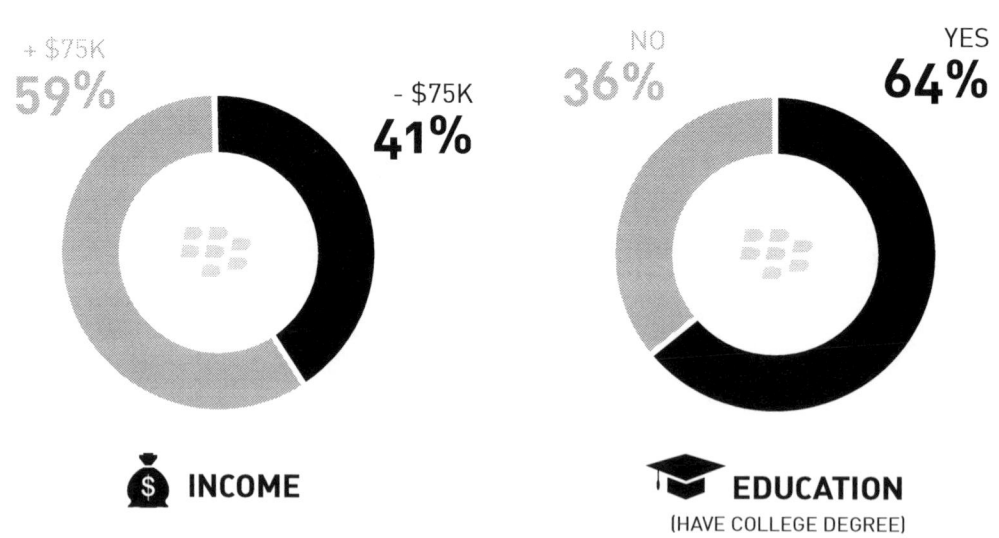

+ $75K
59%

- $75K
41%

INCOME

NO
36%

YES
64%

EDUCATION
(HAVE COLLEGE DEGREE)

WHO HAS WHAT?: COMPARISON

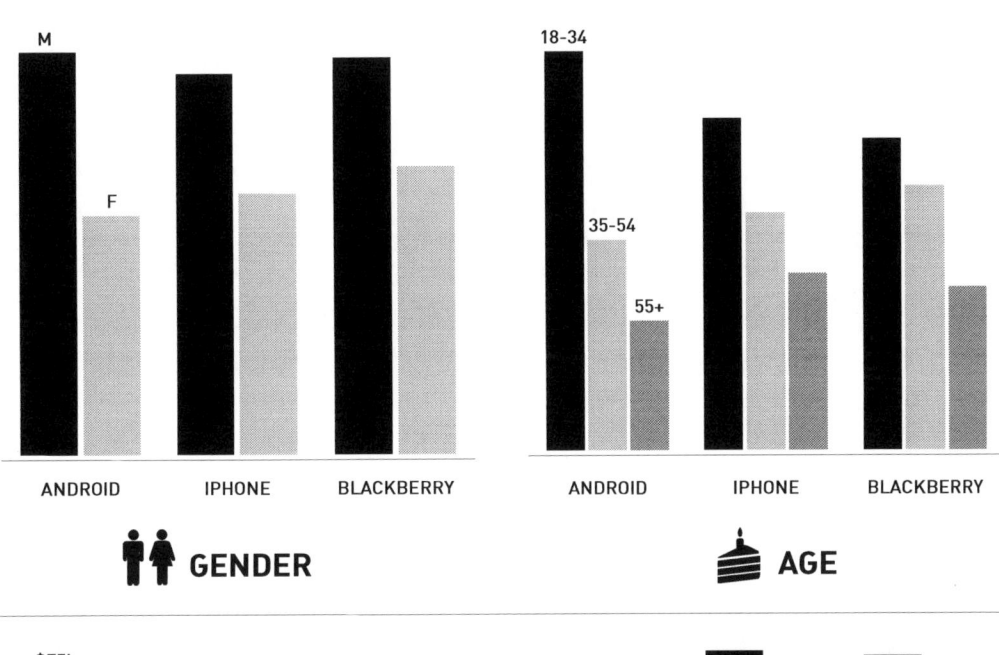

 **GENDER**

AGE

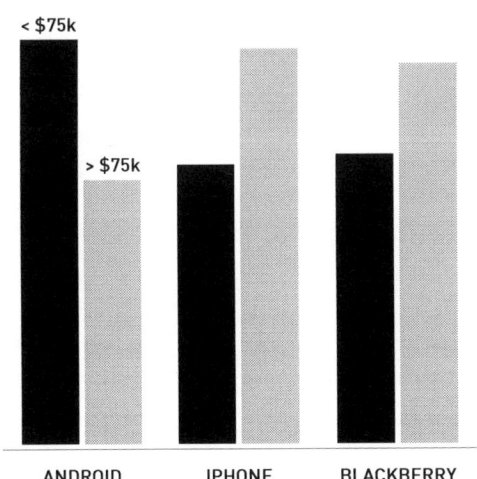

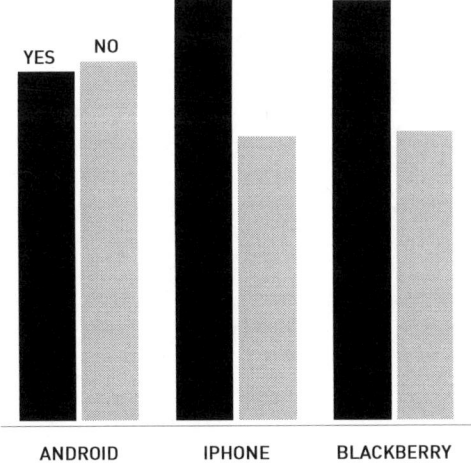

INCOME

 **EDUCATION**
(HAVE COLLEGE DEGREE)

"WHY DON'T WE JUST BUILD A..."

If you are charged with presenting why an app is the right move for your company be sure you're prepared to defend the app versus other end-products.

Why don't we just build a website/microsite/landing page?

- Users carry the app with them all the time and can access it without having internet available.

- An app can be distributed more directly, so only the people you want to have your app can access it.

- App micro environments can be created outside of usual workflows. This can be beneficial for large corporations with lots of red tape or a backed up web department.

Why don't we just build a PDF or other electronic document?

- Apps are easier to distribute—they don't clog up email attachment quotas and don't need a third-party reader to access.

- Apps can push out relevant content and updates and alert the end user in a non-intrusive way when this is complete.

- Apps can be navigated in a number of intuitive ways instead of simply read from front to back or searched.

PART 2 /
UNDERSTANDING APPS

NATIVE VS. HTML5

You will hear this term early on in your project. This is the first Big Decision you will make. Native vs. HTML5—what does that even mean?

Native: This refers to a "native app," meaning an app that is built to work and run on a specific platform. An iPhone native app is designed, built, and released to work on the iPhone (only). If you develop a native app and want it to run on multiple platforms you will have to develop it from the ground up for each platform. (More on that later.)

HTML5: This refers to an app that is built using HTML5/CSS3. Basically it's a website that is designed and developed to work like a native app. These websites (or web apps) work across different devices and platforms.

Hybrids/shell apps: There are additional software packages out there that promise the best of all worlds—one app, multiple platforms. Programs such as PhoneGap and Appcelerator always read like the silver bullet we want: Minimal design/development and maximum coverage and impact.

Well, as of the writing of this book, I've not seen a hybrid/shell app pan out nor have I met anyone who had a good experience using them. The general consensus is that you spend a lot of time learning the systems but end up with something that is just not quite right—regretting the time you dumped into the app-building program when you could have been developing your native app. I anxiously await the point when the market develops a solution that really works, but in my opinion we're not there yet and it's not a good place to spend your time and budget.

Ok, so we've thrown out shell apps as a solution—so now we consider native or HTML5. This will come down to weighing features/functionality/user experience against cost. On the next page you will see several questions to walk you through choosing which way to go. I do suggest you consider these things, but then bring in the firm you are going to work with to build this to help make the final decisions.

Before you jump into the next page though, a recently released study proclaims: *Developers: Up with iOS, down with HTML5*[1] and includes, "It's worth remembering that Facebook CEO Mark Zuckerberg recently said that his biggest mistake to date was betting so heavily on HTML5, and so he's moving the company to native code." While HTML5 may be your best solution from a time and cost perspective, it's always going to be better to go native if you can.

1 Snyder, Bill. "Developers: Up with iOS, down with HTML5 | The Industry Standard - InfoWorld." Business technology, IT news, product reviews and enterprise IT strategies - InfoWorld. Last modified September 27, 2012. Accessed September 30, 2012. http://www.infoworld.com/d/the-industry-standard/developers-ios-down-html5-203393.

A BACKSTORY ABOUT HTML & THE MOON LANDING

HTML (hypertext markup language) is the code language used to make websites. It started as super basic controls—font, color, margins, the ability to make a table.

Pretty soon people got fancy with it and started putting tables together with colors to make a website (like a super formatted Excel file). This soon reached its limitations and CSS (cascading style sheets) were introduced. These allowed more control of how things looked.

From there people started to separate content (HTML) and markup (CSS) so that you could take one content file and make it look very different depending on if you viewed it from a mobile device or a desktop.

Once the smartphone market grew and everyone had these mini computers in their pockets (mini computers with more processing power than the computers they had for the moon landing, no joke![1]) HTML and CSS got major upgrades to do better and fancier things. The latest code base is HTML5 and CSS3. All modern browsers can interpret these code bases, but older browsers don't display them correctly.

---

1 "Space has not changed but technology has, in many cases, improved dramatically. A good example is digital technology where today's cell phones are far more powerful than the computers on the Apollo Command Module and Lunar Module that we used to navigate to the moon and operate all the spacecraft control systems." —Neil Armstrong. Wikiquote. Accessed September 30, 2012. http://en.wikiquote.org/wiki/Neil_Armstrong.

HOW DO YOU CHOOSE BETWEEN A NATIVE AND AN HTML5 APP?

There are several questions to ask yourself and your organization before you make your choice. Below are the six big questions to start with:

1. **Where are your customers?**
   Are they using iPhones, Androids, Windows Mobile, BlackBerrys, or something else? Do they have or need internet access to use your app?

2. **What phone-intrinsic features does your app need?**
   Will it need to access the camera? The maps app? How about storing things on the phone (local storage)?
   Note: More and more features are being opened to HTML5. A great resource is www.caniuse.com to help you understand what is available.

3. **How do you want to distribute your app?**
   Do you need to have it in an app marketplace? Do you need to securely control who can access the data? Is this for internal or external users? Are you going to charge money for your app? Is this a revenue generating idea or a new line of business?

4. **What is your budget?**
   Do you have the money to make the app for the two biggest platforms or do you need to get maximum coverage even if it means sacrificing functionality?

5. **How fast does your app need to be?**
   How important is speed and a smooth user experience? Native apps are much faster and run better than HTML5 and shell apps.

6. **How do you want the app to be updated?**
   Release a new version that users update on their device? Push out new content that automatically refreshes on the device?

What if you can't answer these questions?

Perhaps you just don't know enough yet. Note that you can do both native and HTML apps. It's a great way to get started quickly and gather data. Start with an HTML app to get broad coverage and user testing. Use this to inform which platform to go with first and what features are used most. (This approach only works if your app will have a minimal usable experience in HTML.)

Now (hopefully) you have your boat pointed in the right direction to hit land. The team you work with to create your app can also help you understand these questions in relation to your specific app.

UNDERSTANDING PLATFORMS

Platforms are the different entities you can build your app for.

The main ones are:

- iOS (iPhone/ iPad)

- Android

- BlackBerry

- Windows Phone

- Symbian (Nokia)

The taxonomy in the development chain can be confusing—you can usually just peg one part and say something like, "I want an iPhone and an Android app," although to be totally correct you would say "I want an iOS and an Android app," or "I want an iPhone and an Android mobile app".

The hierarchy of a platform are:

Company → Platform → Development Environment → Distribution → Device.

DEVELOPMENT CHAIN

Development Chain

Company	Google	Apple	RIM	Microsoft	Accenture
Platform	Android	iOS	Blackberry Application Platform	Windows Phone	Symbian
Development Environment	Android SDK (Java)	iOS SDK 4 (Objective C)	Blackberry Java Development Environment (BB JDE)	Windows Phone SDK (.NET)	Qt SDK (C++/others)
Distribution	Google Play Amazon.com: Appstore for Android	App Store (iTunes)	BlackBerry App World	Windows Phone Marketplace	Nokia Store, Ovi
Sample Devices	HTC Droid Incredible Motorola Droid Razr Samsung Galaxy Amazon Kindle Fire	iPod Touch iPhone iPad	Blackberry PlayBook Blackberry Torch Blackberry Bold Blackberry Curve	Nokia Lumina Samsung Focus HTC Arrive	Nokia 808

43

DISTRIBUTION

If you build a native app you will almost certainly distribute it via the app store of that platform (iTunes App Store, Google Play, Amazon App Store, etc). There are just a few things to understand about distribution:

App store distribution – this is the easiest way for people to get your app on their device. They go to a link or find it in an online store and download it and they are done.

Ad hoc distribution – this is difficult, but possible. It's how you can add the app to certain devices only. You cannot do this as a public distribution, but if you are going to a tradeshow or have a meeting and want to show the app before it's publicly available this is a way to do that. There is a limit on how many you apps you can distribute this way (around 100 for iOS).

Business/enterprise distribution – It's also possible to distribute an app securely to only a defined group of people, like employees at a company.

1. 148Apps.biz | iOS development news and information for the community, by the community. "148Apps.biz | Apple iTunes App Store Metrics, Statistics and Numbers for iPhone Apps." Accessed April 22, 2013. http://148apps.biz/app-store-metrics/?mpage=appcount.

2. Wikipedia, the free encyclopedia. "Google Play." Accessed April 22, 2013. http://en.wikipedia.org/wiki/Google_Play.

3. Svetlik , Joe. "Windows Phone Store hits 150,000 apps, doubled in last year." CNET UK. Accessed April 22, 2013. http://crave.cnet.co.uk/software/windows-phone-store-hits-150000-apps-doubled-in-last-year-50010072/.

4. Lunden, Ingrid. "App Stores In Q1 2013 Hauled In $2.2B In Sales On 13.4B Downloads, Google/Apple Duopoly Leading The Way: Canalys | TechCrunch." TechCrunch. Accessed April 22, 2013. http://techcrunch.com/2013/04/08/app-stores-in-q1-2013-hauled-in-2-2b-in-sales-on-13-4b-downloads-googleapple-duopoly-leading-the-way-canalys/.

5. Pradhan, Satyakam. "Amazon Appstore Global Roll-out to Begin Soon, Coming to India as well | Tech Allianz." IT News | Gadget reviews| Techallianz. Accessed April 22, 2013. http://techallianz.info/amazon-appstore-global-roll-out.html.

APPS STORE STATS

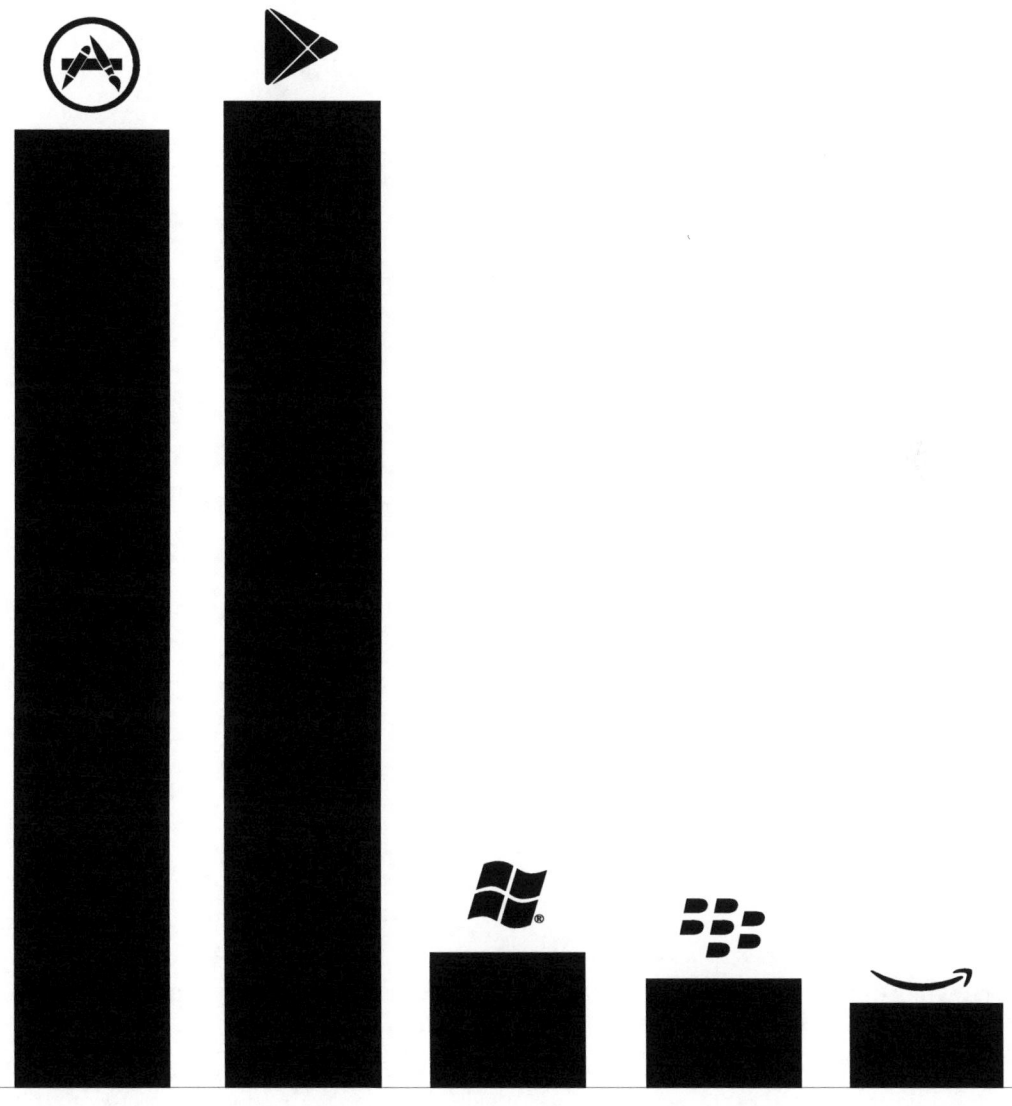

845,000
APPLE STORE
(as of April 2013)[1]

850,000
GOOGLE PLAY
(as of April 2013)[2]

150,000
WINDOWS
MARKETPLACE
(as of Dec 2012)[3]

100,000
BLACKBERRY
APP WORLD
(as of April 2013)[4]

80,000
AMAZON STORE
(as of April 2013)[5]

CHOOSING A PLATFORM

Ok, so time to choose how you will get this done. Where is your audience? Are they on iPhones? Androids? Both? Do you have the time and budget to develop two apps (one for iOS and one for Android) or should you look at doing an HTML5 app?

You may work somewhere that still issues BlackBerrys—and have seen people carrying two or more devices with them. There is a huge BYOD (bring your own device) movement happening in corporate America, so don't necessarily go off your corporate policy when picking a platform.

But how do you really know what your customers are using? Well, talk to them. Review the Google Analytics on your website (it now includes a section for mobile, so you can see what people are using).

This book outlines building an iOS app and building an Android app (plus a section on HTML5 apps). These are the two platforms most people focus on. Why is that? You look at BlackBerry—it used to dominate corporate America, and still has highly educated, older, affluent customers and wonder why any professional business wouldn't develop for this company. While your company may decide that BlackBerry, Windows Phone, or Symbian are worth the development costs, here are the reasons I hear (and give) the most for not working on them:

- Developers and designers are steering away from BlackBerry because of all the buttons. Some BlackBerrys have arrow buttons, some have a scroll wheel, some are touch screen. You have to code your app for every input instance. See the next page for some examples. The iPhone has one button—and that button doesn't interact with the app. Android has a couple buttons (back and menu) and those interactions are straightforward.

- You have to make your money work for you. Creating a second version of your app for another platform won't cost the same as developing first version; it's going to be substantially more once you leave the world of iOS and Android. Is that small extra market share worth that kind of cost? Even when those market shares decrease almost every quarter?

- It's extremely difficult to find a developer for anything but the big two. And if you find one developer and that person doesn't work out or moves on, can you possibly find another one?

- It's incredibly unclear on what is going to happen with Windows Phone. Windows Phone just isn't picking up market share like it was promised to do. As a developer, would you take your career in a path that could dry up completely or would you focus on the growth platforms?

Storm2 9550

P'9981

Curve 8350i

Bold 9930

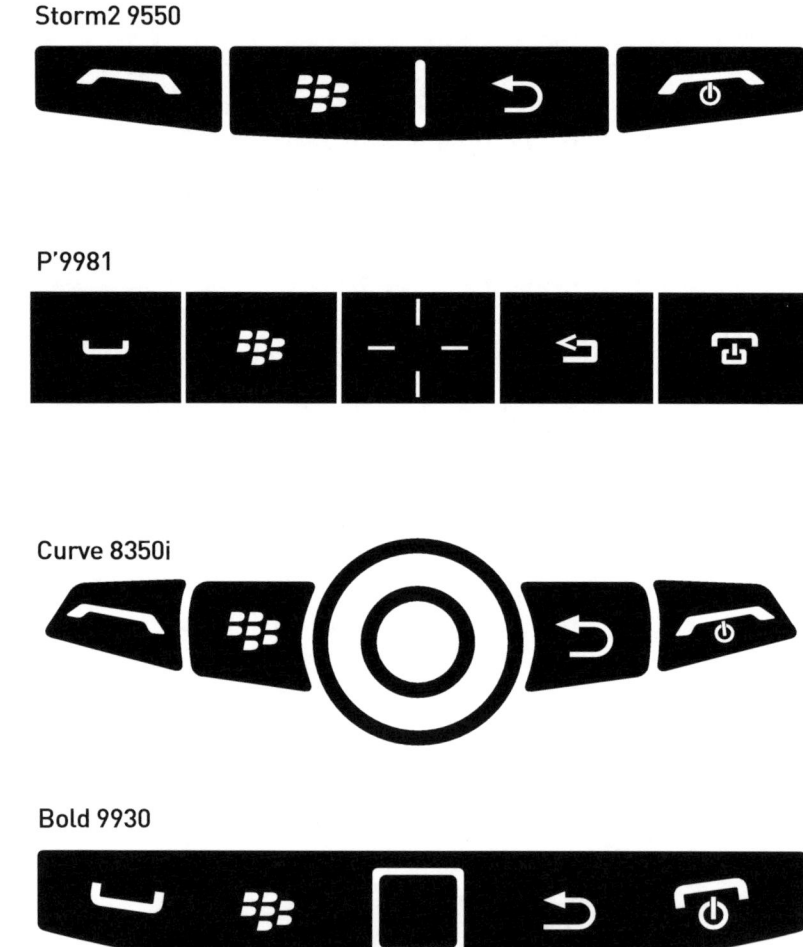

Different button configurations on current-model BlackBerry smartphones [1]

1 "BlackBerry - Smartphones - New BlackBerry Phones - Touch Phones from BlackBerry - CA - US." BlackBerry
   - Official BlackBerry - Tablets - Smartphones - Cell Phones - Mobile Phones - Apps at BlackBerry - US.
   Accessed August 26, 2012. http://us.blackberry.com/smartphones.html?CPID=KNC-kw379015_p6&HBX_
   PK=rim%7C78c3a4fd-17b3-2ca9-4bc5-00004ab56ded.

RESOLUTION: A TALE OF PIXELS AND DENSITIES

Before we go into the two main platforms there are a couple heady concepts to understand when talking about screen resolution. You would like to think this stuff is only for designers and developers, but this whole section is focused on you—so stick with me here.

Resolution is used to mean both size and density—how large the screen is (in pixels) and how many pixels are packed into an inch (pixels per inch, or ppi).

Why are you being barraged with all this information? Well, the moral of the story is that you have to accept each device as its own little world and expect that your app will look good on one device, but different on another one. One figure puts 1,363 device models running Android (on 599 different brands). This is called fragmentation[1], and the fact is that you cannot possibly test your app on every device out there. Especially when dealing with the resolutions of Android you need to give more broad comments such as, "Align all these elements" instead of, "Move this icon 2 pixels to the left." See page 52 for an example of brand fragmentation on Android.

---

1   Arthur, Charles, and Stuart Dredge. "iOS v Android: why Schmidt was wrong and developers still start on Apple | Technology | guardian.co.uk." Latest US news, world news, sport and comment from the Guardian | guardiannews.com | The Guardian. Last modified June 10, 2012. Accessed August 10, 2012. http://www.guardian.co.uk/technology/appsblog/2012/jun/10/apple-developer-wwdc-schmidt-android.

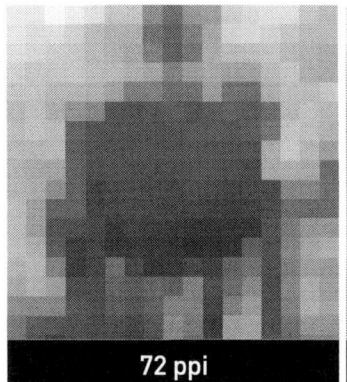

72 ppi　　136 ppi　　362 ppi

Resolution is used to mean both size and density—how large the screen is (in pixels) and how many pixels are packed into an inch (pixels per inch, or ppi).

px: pixels

ppi: pixels per square inch

Size: 72px x 72px
Density: 9ppi

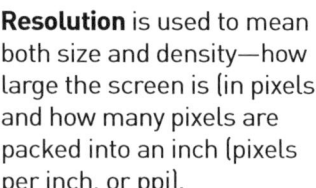

Size: 72px x 72px
Density: 18ppi

Size: 144px x 144px
Density: 9ppi

Size: 72px x 72px
Density: 18ppi

Android Options

Screen Size	Low Density 120 ldpi	Medium Density 160 mdpi	High Density 160 hdpi	Extra High Density 160 hdpi
Small Screen	240x320		480x640	
Normal Screen	240x400 240x432	320x480	480x800 480x854 600x1024	640x960
Large Screen	480x800 480x845	480x800 480x854 600x1024		
Extra Large Screen	1024x600	1280x800 1024x768 1280x768	1536x1152 1920x1152 1920x1600	2048x1536 2560x1536 2560x1600

iOS Options

Screen Size	Standard iPhone: 136 ppi iPad: 132 ppi iPad Mini: 163 ppi	Retina iPhone: 362 ppi iPad: 264 ppi
iPhone	320x468	640x960 640x1136
iPad	1024x768	2048x1536
iPad Mini	1024x768	

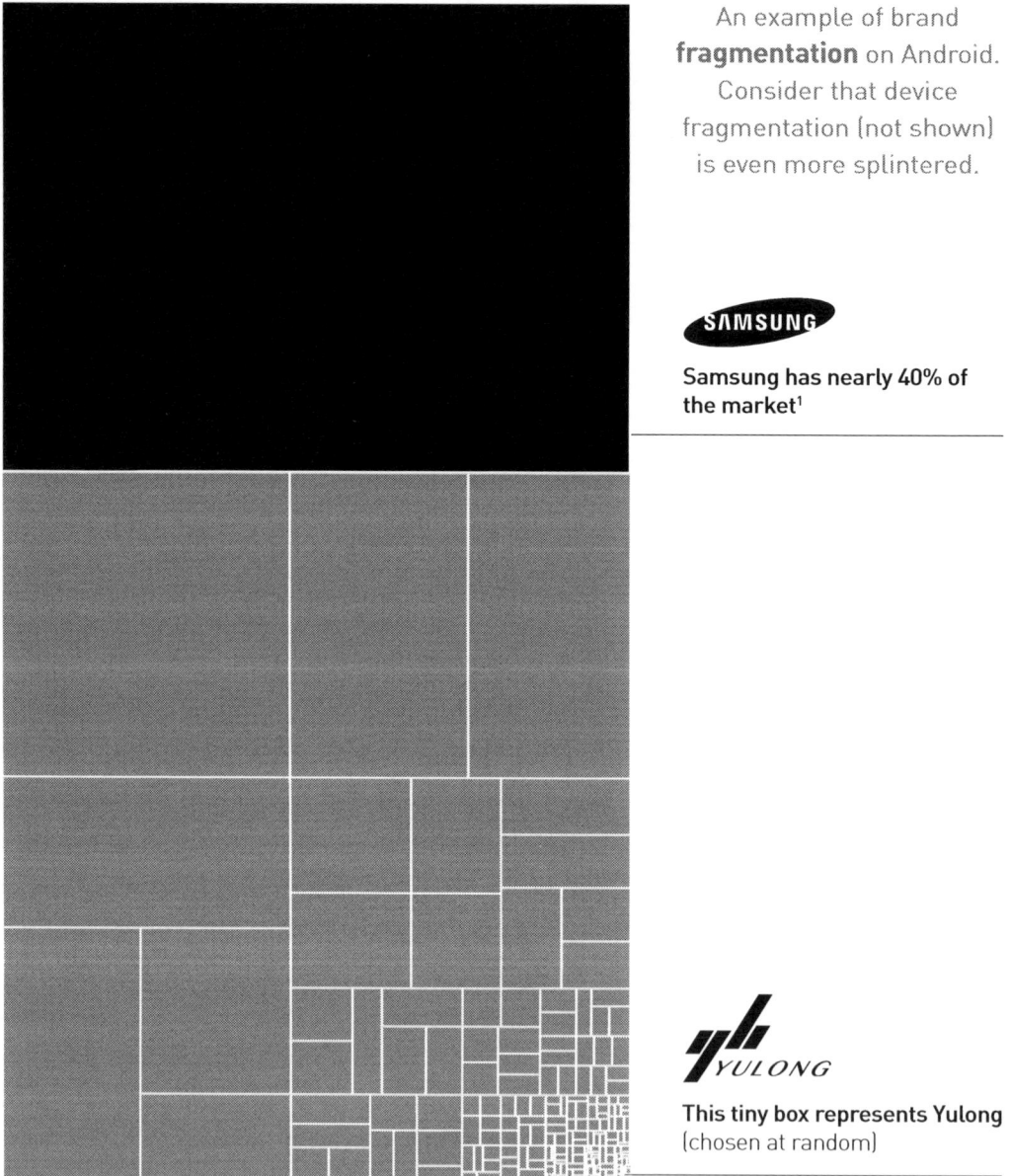

An example of brand **fragmentation** on Android. Consider that device fragmentation (not shown) is even more splintered.

SAMSUNG

Samsung has nearly 40% of the market[1]

YULONG

This tiny box represents Yulong (chosen at random)

1 "OpenSignalMaps - Android Fragmentation Visualized." OpenSignalMaps - Cell Phone Tower and Signal Heat Maps. Accessed August 10, 2012. http://opensignal.com/reports/fragmentation.php.

BUILDING AN IOS APP

iOS is the operating system used on iPhone and iPad. Apple owns everything in this process—the hardware, the software, and the app stores. One entity owning it means that things are very standardized and controlled.

Here is a short list of things to know:

- There are two resolutions of iPhone—standard display and Retina display. Standard display is almost unsupported by now as it's only on older phones. See the Resolutions section for more information.

- There are two resolutions of iPad—standard display and Retina display. Both still need to be supported.

- iPhones through the 4S model had the same size screen, but the iPhone 5 introduced a new (taller) screen.

- All iPhones have a camera. iPad 1 does not have a camera but iPad 2 and the new iPad do.

- Apple encourages developers to only make and support the latest iOS version. You may need to consider the limitations and fall backs of your app (for instance, if you have an app that takes pictures, add an error code for iPad 1 users), but you do not need to plan to support more than one version of your app.

- Designers need to provide up to five versions of each graphic, although you can save some time by reusing the exact same size graphics from iPhone with Retina display to the standard iPad.

- There are only a handful of fonts installed in iOS that can be used in apps; however, you can load any TrueType font into your app to use something besides the standard ones.

- You release one bundled app that contains the iPhone and iPad version.

- You can offer your app on sale, but you cannot give copies away, do a free trial, or offer coupons/discounts to the public. You can, however, give out a few promo codes (currently the max is 50 codes per app version). The way people get around this is to release a lite version with less functionality so people can try before they buy or rely on making money via in-app purchases.

- To release an app you must have an Apple Developers License. To get your license you need to apply and pay an annual fee of $99. The application takes a couple weeks. You can start that process at developer.apple.com.

- As a client you can become an Apple Developer even if you aren't the developer—your development firm just needs to release it under your name/license instead of theirs (you will need to give them access to do so). If you charge for your app, you will probably want to hold the license, since the money earned goes to the licensed entity. Most firms will cut you a check each month if it's under their license, but they will also probably charge you a processing percentage to do so.

- Apple takes about a week to review apps. Each new app and update must be submitted for review. If something is rejected, plan to fix it and wait another week. Once it's approved it's in the App Store in about 24 hours. Be aware of blackout dates for review (around holidays and major releases).

For extensive information refer to the iOS Human Interface Guidelines at developer.apple.com.

APPLE RECEIVES 30 PERCENT OF EVERYTHING.

You need to understand this at your very core. From the purchase price to in-app purchases, Apple earns 30 percent.

In-app purchases are anything you can possibly buy in the app, not just app upgrades. In-app purchases could be a membership to your site or products you are selling—even if they don't have anything to do with the app, Apple will still earn 30 percent.

You can lament this all day and even throw a little temper tantrum, but it won't change their mind. Ever notice how you can't actually buy anything from the Amazon app? Be careful if you build a Point of Access app (see page 15) to a membership or other account-based site, because unless it's done in a clever way you are about to share 30 percent of your income with Apple.

IOS VERSIONS

As of the writing of this book, iOS 6.0 was just released. Apple all but forces you to upgrade your software regularly and discourages developers from developing for obsolete versions.

Apple only has one version of iOS in play at a time, and that version is installed on all upgraded iPhones, iPads, iPod Touches, and Apple TVs. In fact, just a week after the new software was released 60% of all iPhone users and 41% of iPad users were already on the new software version[1].

For a more complete list of operating system versions visit http://en.wikipedia.org/wiki/IOS_version_history.

---

1 Etherington, Darrell. "iOS 6 Adoption At Just Over One Week: 60% For iPhone And 41% For iPad | TechCrunch." TechCrunch. Last modified September 28, 2012. Accessed September 29, 2012. http://techcrunch.com/2012/09/28/ios-6-adoption-at-just-over-one-week-60-for-iphone-and-41-for-ipad/.

Designing for iOS

This is information your designer will use to create graphics for iOS. It's helpful if you have a basic understanding of it.

iPhone apps should be designed at Retina display size and graphics reduced (using Nearest Neighbor in Photoshop) 50 percent for standard display.

Everything possible in an app should be a placed vector graphic or built using the shape tool. Rasters are the enemy and will only cause you pain.

Set up Photoshop correctly

Make sure that when you design for Retina display by default everything is in the power of 2 (2 pixel lines, 10 pixel drop shadows, etc), because reducing to standard cuts everything in half (your 2 pixel line will appear to be a 1 pixel line).

Set up your grid so the minimum grid lines are 2 pixels. Do this in Photoshop → Preferences → Guides, Grid & Slices.

In the Grid section, set "Gridline Every" to 20 pixels and the Subdivisions to 2.

Turn on Snap To → All to keep everything aligned to the grid.

Naming files

There are four size/resolution combos of each graphic that can be provided (see page 51). The file naming convention is as follows:

If your slice name is "logo", your file names would be:

- logo~iphone.png

- logo@2x~iphone.png

- logo~ipad.png

- logo@2x~ipad.png

DESIGNING FOR IOS (CONTINUED)

However, if your logo is the same size on iPhone with Retina display and the standard iPad, and you aren't supporting iPhone with standard display, your files would just be:

- logo.png (iPhone Retina display, iPad standard display, no iPhone standard display)

- logo@2x~ipad.png (iPad Retina display

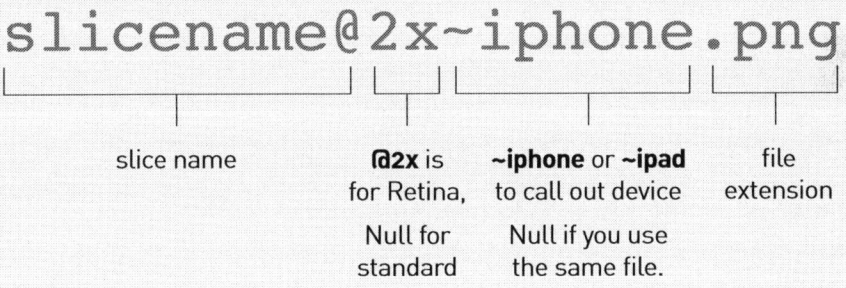

| slice name | @2x is for Retina, Null for standard | ~iphone or ~ipad to call out device Null if you use the same file. | file extension |

DEVELOPING FOR IOS

The language used for iOS is Objective-C. It is pretty much limited to iOS and OS X (the operating system on desktop/laptop Apple products). It derives similarities from C and Smalltalk.

Developers use an application named X-Code to develop iOS apps. X-Code is free and available from Apple.

There is a great app called TestFlight that allows you to send out versions of your app with release notes to testers without them having to provide their UDID (because no client in the world gets that done easily).

BUILDING AN ANDROID APP

There are hundreds of Android devices. They come in different resolutions, different levels of quality, different versions, and all price ranges. It's this open system that has contributed to the rapid spread of the Android platform—but it creates some issues with getting the design and development just right.

Here is a short list of things to know:

» To really understand Android read through their developer portal: http://developer.android.com. This isn't just for coders; it goes through philosophy, design, and development. Once a year there is a huge Google event called Google I/O—you can see what was covered in that event on the developer portal. The event will cover new releases and have the most current Android information.

» There are several different app stores you can list your app in. The main ones are Google Play (formerly Android Marketplace) and Amazon App store for Android.

» You can offer your app on sale, but you cannot give a copy away, do a free trial, or offer a coupon/discount. The way people get around this is to release a lite version with less functionality so people can try before they buy or rely on making money via in-app purchases.

» Amazon will receive 30 percent of all app sales and in-app purchases through the Amazon App Store.

» You will weep buckets of tears if you try to develop and support an app for Kindle or Kindle Fire. They have tweaked their versions of Android and made it difficult to develop for. However, this may change soon. Amazon is making strides to make it easier to build for and may end-of-life these devices soon and introduce a new model.

ANDROID VERSIONS

As of the writing of this book Jelly Bean (4.1.x) is in production. This is the first version that is for both mobile and tablet devices. Developers still need to support Ice Cream Sandwich (4.0.x for mobile) and Honeycomb (3.x.x for tablets).

Android users don't upgrade their operating systems as quickly as iOS users, though (see page 55). This is partially because Google allows device manufacturers and service carriers to decide if and when to push out an update[1]. The most popular operating system still being used is Gingerbread—released in 2010—see the full breakdown, next page.

For a more complete list of operating system versions visit http://en.wikipedia.org/wiki/Android_(operating_system).

1 Rowinski, Dan. "Why You May Not Be Getting the Latest Android Update Anytime Soon." ReadWriteWeb - Web Apps, Web Technology Trends, Social Networking and Social Media. Last modified July 2, 2012. Accessed September 29, 2012. http://www.readwriteweb.com/mobile/2012/07/why-you-may-not-be-getting-the-latest-android-update-anytime-soon.php.

2 Johnston, Casey. "Android 4.0 leaps to 16 percent install base, version 4.1 at 0.8 percent | Ars Technica." Ars Technica. Last modified August 2, 2012. Accessed September 10, 2012. http://arstechnica.com/gadgets/2012/08/android-4-0-leaps-to-16-percent-install-base-version-4-1-at-0-8-percent/.

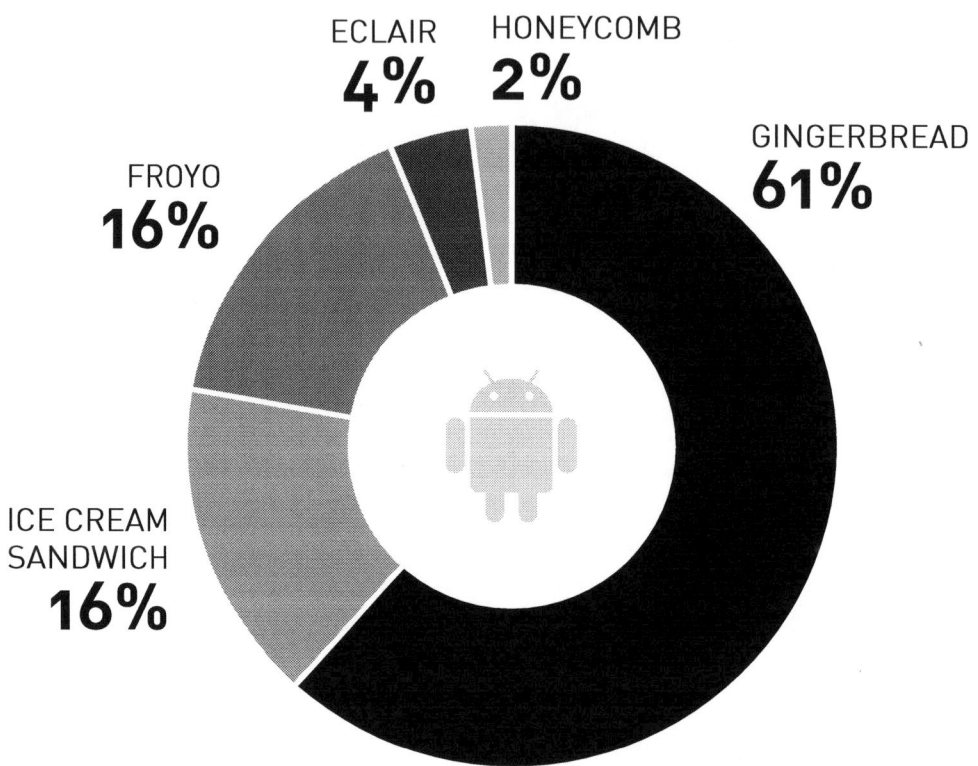

ECLAIR
4%

HONEYCOMB
2%

GINGERBREAD
61%

FROYO
16%

ICE CREAM
SANDWICH
16%

CONTAINS LESS THAN 2% OF CUPCAKE, DONUT, AND JELLY BEAN

Android operating system installations

Android users are slow to upgrade their operating systems, either
because they choose not to or (more likely) device manufacturers
and carriers don't make these updates available.

DESIGNING FOR ANDROID

This is information your designer will use to create graphics for Android. It's helpful if you have a basic understanding of it.

Start by visiting the Android Developer portal, which has a design section: developer.android.com.

Android is very fluid. We recommend designing a mobile version at 320 px by 480 px with medium density and a tablet version at 1280 x 800 at extra-high density (that's the size of a Samsung Galaxy Tab 10.1). This will help you design for an average size, but you may want to consider the extremely small versions as well.

There are four sizes and four resolutions for Android (see page 51).

Android encourages you to use design Patterns. These are consistent layouts that help people quickly understand how to use your app. Head over to the developer portal and pay close attention to the Patterns section.

DEVELOPING FOR ANDROID

The language used for Android is Java. Developers may have learned this by working on projects such as client server web applications, intranet applications, or some embedded systems.

Developers use an application named Eclipse or other integrated development environment (IDE) that supports Java to develop Android apps.

BUILDING AN HTML5/WEB APP

Unlike developing apps on specific platforms, an HTML5/web app is basically a self-contained website that uses app-like user interface features. You can (and should) hide the browser elements, create a launch icon, and mimic native apps pretty closely.

Here is a short list of things to know:

- A good web designer/developer can create an HTML5 web app—this is the language they are used to, just a different format.

- Don't forget all the ancillary items you will need to make this sing like a native app— home screen launch icons, start screens, etc.

- Web apps are built on percentages and are fluid to fit a variety of devices. This is also called Responsive Design, although that term is used more to indicate a website that will work on desktop, mobile device, and tablet.

- We normally design and support portrait orientation (only) for mobile devices, and landscape and portrait for tablet and landscape desktop.

- You can distribute your app like any website—provide a link and let people go. You cannot put an HTML5 app in any of the app stores unless you wrap it in a framework. Your users will have to visit a website and choose to add a bookmark or add the icon to their home screen. You can add prompts in the app to encourage or force them to do this.

SUPPORTED BROWSERS

To make an HTML5 app you have to make some browser sacrifices. You just aren't going to support Internet Explorer 6...or 7...or maybe even 8. You are only going to support the modern browsers that can handle the code you are writing.

You are probably also not going to support Silk, the browser used on Kindles and Kindle Fires. It doesn't hold to spec because Amazon has tweaked the hell out of it.

These are the browsers that need to be supported:

Browsers to Support	
🌐 **Web Browsers**	☐ **Mobile Browsers**
IE 9+	Android Jelly Bean
Safari 5+	Android Ice Cream Sandwich
Chrome 16+	Android Honeycomb
Firefox 13+	iOS 6+

DESIGNING FOR HTML5

This is information your designer will use to create graphics for HTML5 apps. It's helpful if you have a basic understanding of it.

You have to figure out what constitutes a "desktop," a "mobile," and a "tablet." We call these "break points" and use these sizes:

- Desktop: 960px and larger[1]

- Tablet Landscape: 800px – 1024px[2]

- Tablet Portrait: 600px – 800px

- Mobile (Portrait only): < 600px[3]

Choose if you will support Retina display graphics and if you will also supply smaller graphics. Remember, while bandwidth access on desktops is usually very fast for business and residential connections, bandwidth via cellular networks is much slower still and image sizes and page load times need to be considered for mobile devices.

1 Yes, people have very large desktops (mine is 2560px x 1440 px) so you can break free of the 960 grid; however, unless your app really needs and can use more space, consider that most people use larger monitors to have several windows open at a time, not to see bigger websites.

2 You have to make a decision for all the 7" tablets out there—we serve the mobile version for portrait and the tablet version for landscape for these screens.

3 We include a density factor to make sure we catch Retina display iPhones which the browser will pick up as tablet sized without this.

DEVELOPING FOR HTML5

The languages used for a web app are HTML5, CSS3, and Javascipt. Javascript is normally used with a framework; a popular one is jQuery. Developers may have learned this by working on other web projects.

PRICING AN APP

There are lots of ways to price your app. Will it be free because it's a marketing expense? Will you charge for it to earn revenue?

How you price your app depends on where it falls in your organization. There are a few things to know as you think about pricing. You cannot do a discount code or free for some/paid for others (although you can gift an app, which you still pay for). Some apps put out a "lite" version with limited functionality to help convince people to buy the paid one.

There is a strategy about free apps and then making your money via in-app purchases (also called freemium). I'll let the graphs[1] do the talking:

72% of revenue:
comes from apps featuring in-app purchases

---

1 Etherington, Darrell. "The App Store hurtles toward a freemium-focused future — Apple News, Tips and Reviews." GigaOM. Last modified September 20, 2011. Accessed September 10, 2012. http://gigaom.com/apple/the-app-store-hurtles-toward-a-freemium-focused-future/.

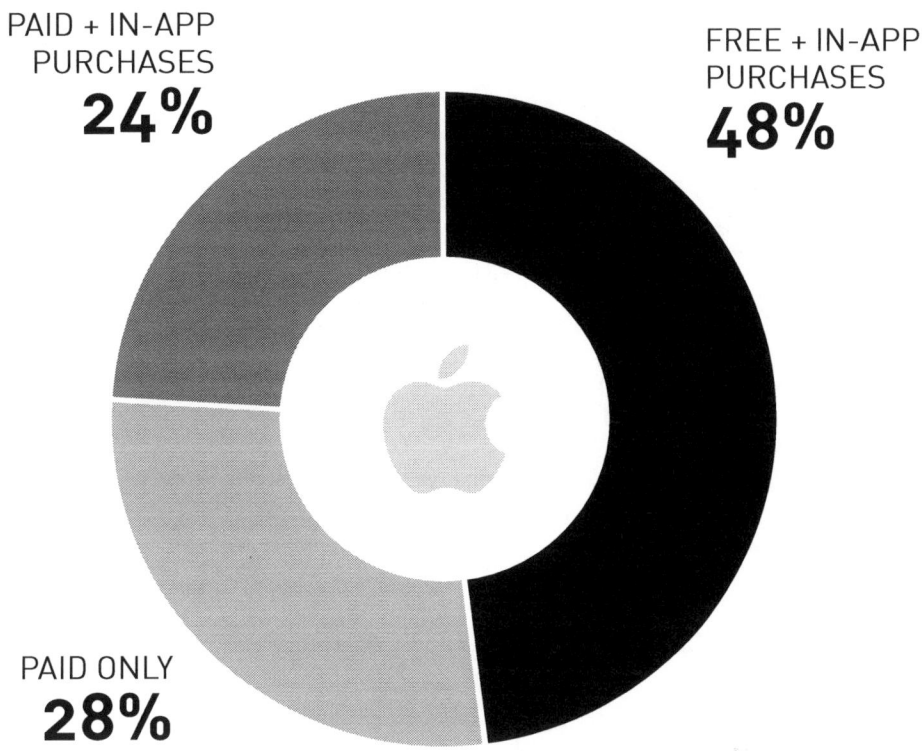

PAID + IN-APP
PURCHASES
24%

FREE + IN-APP
PURCHASES
48%

PAID ONLY
28%

Revenue sources
Your best bet? Offering a free app with in-app purchases.

PART 3 /
GETTING YOUR APP BUILT

WHAT DOES AN APP COST TO BUILD?

Ah, pricing. It can feel like black magic. Since everyone keeps their pricing close to the vest, I can only share my own firm's philosophy and what I was able to find online.

First of all, (spoiler alert) apps are more expensive than websites. We learned some hard lessons here. At first we thought an app was just a slightly different sized website from a design perspective and a slightly different programming language from a development perspective.

If you even just skimmed the sections about resolution and building an iOS or Android app you start to see the issues. Apps have a lot of extra work to make them run, from the different icons to several sizes of the same graphic to the gestures and functionality built. Not to mention if you build an iOS app and an Android app you have to start from scratch in a different programming language for each and tweak the design for each.

And there are even more things to consider that affect price:[1]

- What kind of infrastructure do you need?

- Will you also need a server or are you looking to do local storage?

- What other systems might this tie into?

- How will your app talk to your other business tools?

- Will it be through an API?

- Does that API need to be written or revised to work with the app?

This is What Factors Into Our Pricing:

- How complex the app is—does it do a lot of things or just serve up some information?

- How much functionality is built—and is that functionality standard on the platform?

- How will the client handle updates—will we push information or issue a downloadable update?

Beyond that there are some subjective issues that are taken into account when bidding a job:

- How busy the firm is—do we need to cut a little leaner to get the project to fill empty slots or are we so in demand we can't even think about it unless we are willing to work nights and weekends?

- How much there is to learn—do we know all the solutions and have built them before (and can reuse code), or do we need to try to figure this out on a wing and a prayer?

---

1 This article helped flush out my list: Nguyen, Kent. "Dear business people, an iOS app actually takes a lot of work!." Blog | Kent Nguyen. Last modified January 31, 2012. Accessed August 10, 2012. http://kentnguyen.com/ios/what-does-it-take-to-make-an-ios-app/.

- Are we experts—is this a field or project we are well versed in? Does the client reap huge gains by hiring our expertise in this field or project?

- Do we want to do this—is this project fun? Does it fulfill a need or a desire we have?

- What does the project mean for the client — is this a tiny little internal project for a favorite client or is this a huge revenue-generating strategy?

- What is the client relationship—are the clients good partners or are they selfish/demanding/uneducated?

- How many meetings are needed—is this a standard weekly meeting job? Do the meetings have to be in person? Do we have to drive to the next county and lose three hours a week?

- How much do we "feel" like this should cost—this is usually the number we start with and often the number our other figures come out to. It's something that firms that have done this for a long time can nail confidently.

"OK, FINE, BUT GIVE ME SOME NUMBERS."

This is the hardest part, right? Sharing the actual numbers without knowing more about a project. There is also a fear from firms that we'll give you some numbers to work with and we'll be asked to hold to them even though the project is a totally different beast. Here goes:

The bare minimum we can look at for a single-platform, single-form-factor (so only an iPhone app) is about $5,000.

Mid-sized apps are between $15,000 and $60,000 with some apps going into the $150,000 range.

Those are huge ranges—we know that. Can you get it done cheaper? Probably, but you get what you pay for. Can it cost more? Absolutely, the limit to your imagination is only your budget.

What about developers in India, Bulgaria, or Argentina? They are definitely out there and would love the work. However, our firm only works with US-based designers and developers. We think the money should be reinvested in the local economy through the purchase of coffees and lunches and the payment of local taxes.

Expect to pay some amount up front (maybe 30 percent) with the balance due on completion or submission to the app stores, or expect to make incremental payments and then the balance due. You can negotiate this structure—some firms charge 50 percent up front and 50 percent on delivery. We had a project that was 40 percent up front, 10 percent each month for the next three months, 25 percent on completion and the last 5 percent two weeks after launch (to make sure we cleaned up any trailing issues). This worked well for everyone on a high-dollar project.

DON'T TAKE MY WORD FOR IT

There are a few other brave souls that have echoed this pricing, and end up on roughly the same range as we do. One of the most interesting ones I read answered the 'how much' question with 'it costs as much as a car does, it just depends on what you want'. Are you looking for a 1994 Honda Civic or a late model Audi Q7, or do you really want a Lamborghini Aventador?

I've been collecting a list of prices for the last year or so and with this update of the book comes several new sources, but sings the same tune:

Cost of Building an App

Minimum	Mid-Sized	Average	High End	Src
$3,000 very bare minimum	$35,000 for low/average complexity	$30,000 – $40,000 average cost of an app	$150,000 larger app (two developers, four months)	1
$1,000 – $4,000 development only simple, table based app	$8,000 – $50,000 development only database app (native)	$10,000 – $250,000 development only games	**Development add-ons** $1,000 – $3,000 in-app purchasing + $1,000 – $5,000 web services + $1,000 Game Center + $500–1,500 share capabilities	2
	$500–10,000 design iPhone standard (25% more for Retina; 50% more for iPad)			
$1,000 – $5,000 1994 Honda Civic simple app	$20,000 – $25,000 2007 BMW 335i solid one platform	$50,000 – $75,000 Audi Q7 works on anything	$400,000+ Lamborghini the very best...	3
N/A	$20,000	$35,000	$150,000	4
$1,500 – $5,000	$10,000	$30,000	$150,000	5*

1 Dilworth, Dianna. "How Much Does It Cost To Make An Android App? - AppNewser." mediabistro.com: jobs, classes, community and news for media professionals. Last modified May 7, 2012. Accessed August 12, 2012. http://www.mediabistro.com/appnewser/how-much-does-it-cost-to-make-an-android-app_b22641.

2 Carter. "How Much Does It Cost To Develop an App | iPhone App Development Costs." iPhone App Marketing | Bluecloud Solutions | How To Make Money With Apps. Accessed September 29, 2012. http://www.bluecloudsolutions.com/blog/cost-develop-app/.

3 Lakas, Alex. "DarwinApps • Q: "How much does an app cost?" A: "About as much as a car."." DarwinApps. Accessed April 22, 2013. http://blog.darwinapps.com/post/36041399961/appcostscar.

4 Stangarone, Joe. "How much does native mobile app development cost? | mrc's Cup of Joe Blog." Enterprise Web Application Development | Web Application Development Software | Database Application Development. Accessed April 22, 2013. http://www.mrc-productivity.com/blog/2013/02/how-much-does-native-mobile-app-development-cost/.

5 "develop app cost - How much does it really cost developing an app?" Accessed April 22, 2013. http://createownapps.com/2013/01/develop-app-cost/. *includes infographic*

HOW TO HIRE A FIRM

So, you have your ducks in a row and you understand some things about apps (including that it's going to cost some money to get one). Now what?

Now you find a firm or an individual or two. Find someone you want to work with. Find a good partner, because you are going to spend some quality time together. Grade this partner on:

- How much you like them personally.

- How well they present themselves.

- How they communicate (both timeliness and demeanor).

- What is in their portfolio.

- If you feel like the price for the project is a good value.

Do not just compare on price alone, because price is nothing when you are compare eating a fast-food hamburger in your car to enjoying a meal at your favorite restaurant with your favorite person.

WHAT TO LOOK FOR

- You need a solid designer (or designers).

- You need a solid developer who writes the language of your platform.

- You need a project manager/account rep.

You may find this combination in just two people—a designer who is also the project manager or a developer who is also an account rep. Some developers will write code for multiple platforms, but most are only fluent in one so you will need a developer per platform.

Be extremely careful if you find all this in one person. A designer who is great at user interfaces can rarely code at this level and the developer who can make it work could have no sense of aesthetics. If you do find this one person, make sure to really dig into their previous apps and ask them to be specific about doing 100 percent of it themselves. They are out there, but so is the Hope Diamond.

DO YOU NEED AN APP-SPECIFIC DESIGNER/DEVELOPER?

If you have a firm or a person you love working with but they aren't specifical-ly an app designer or developer, should you work with them? Absolutely! Apps have only been around a few years—great designers and developers have been around for decades. As long as they are willing to put in the time it takes to learn how to do it (assuming they already have the background and you have the time/budget), then trust them.

If you have an in-house person at a large corporation it's important to bring them in on this decision. An in-house designer who mainly does print work may not have the expertise or desire to become an app designer. It's as differ-ent as a mechanic and a race car driver—just because they both work with cars doesn't mean they know or want to learn how to be the other person. The same thing goes for your developers—just because they write C# doesn't mean they write Objective-C, or want to learn how.

BEFORE YOU START LOOKING

Before you call the first firm on your hit list you should have a few things in order. You don't have to be formal about this, but at the bare minimum you should know:

- Roughly what your app should do.

- Roughly what your budget will be.

- About when you need it.

You can take this to a whole other level and fill out a creative brief and have all of this documented. Although, we recommend having your firm involved in this step, so that you are relying on their expertise in building apps and not using them only as production workers. If you do want to go ahead without them, here are the things we normally ask on a first-fact finding mission[1]:

---

1 Our project planner is based on the one used at Happy Cog, which they encourage everyone to use, "Feel free to borrow anything you see in there, as we feel it's for the greater good," so you will see a lot of firms using it.

Hoy, Greg. "A List Apart: Articles: RFPs: The Least Creative Way to Hire People." A List Apart. Last modified July 5, 2011. Accessed December 12, 2012 http://www.alistapart.com/articles/rfps-the-least-creative-way-to-hire-people/.

WORKSHEET: APP PLANNING 1 / 5

Background information

- How did you learn about our firm? Did you find us in search or were you referred (we want to thank our referrer)? Did you attend an event we spoke at? Did you read something we published?

- Have you been through an app design / development effort before? If yes, what role did you play?

About your organization

- What does your organization do? Why does it matter?

- How large/how mature is your company?

- How many people would be involved in this project at your organization?

- Is your organization receptive to working with vendors remotely (understanding at certain points face-to-face meetings may be necessary)?

About your project

- What type of project are you looking to do?

- What platform(s) are you looking to release on?

- Is this a redesign of an existing project, or a new project altogether?

- Describe the concept, project, or service this app is intended to provide or promote.

- What are some of the fundamental issues you're trying to improve or business problems you're trying to solve with this app?

- What apps do you consider competitors? Please comment on their strengths and/or weaknesses.

- Aside from competitors, are there any apps you consider best-of-breed? (Could be completely outside of your business or industry.)

- What differentiates your project or idea from the competition?

- Who on your end will guide this project to completion?

- Who will be responsible for maintaining the project after launch?

About your audience

- To the best of your ability, describe the primary and secondary users of your app.

- What known needs are they bringing to your app? (Examples include: Curiosity about or passionate interest in subject matter, desire to help a cause/become involved, business need requiring software solution.)

- Into what general demographic or user groups do they fall? (Examples of user groups on an educational site might include parents, teachers, students, donors, and alumni.)

- For the purposes of this new app or redesign, which of these groups are most important?

- What primary action should a primary user take when visiting/using your app? (Examples include: Registering for an account, using it as a tool, playing a game, reading information.)

- What user needs does your existing app fulfill?

- What needs aren't being met? Where does the app fall short?

- If this is a redesign, why else do you seek a redesign? Has your app undergone formal or informal usability testing?

About your brand

- Describe in as few words as possible the feelings you wish your app to evoke, and the brand attributes you want it to convey. (Sample feelings might include: warmth, friendliness, reassurance, comfort, or excitement. Sample brand attributes might include: caring, honesty, humor, professionalism, intelligence, technological savvy, sophistication, reliability, and trustworthiness.)

- Using adjectives and short phrases, describe the app's desired look and feel. (Easy to use, edgy, classic, up-to-date, crisp, modern, traditional, understated, etc.)

- Do you have a visual identity established, or is that something you need designed or evolved?

Features & scope

- Does your plan include community or social features, such as user profiles, commenting, RSS feeds, forums, sharing, friend lists, rating/voting, user-generated content, social media (Facebook, Pinterest, Tumblr, Instagram, Twitter, LinkedIn), etc.?

APP PLANNING WORKSHEET

- Does your plan include media-intensive components such as video, audio, podcasts, and other rich media?

- Are you looking for the redesigned/new app to be powered by a content management system or publishing platform?

- Are there any third-party integration points we need to know about (interfaces to a CRM, e-commerce, mapping solution, social site, or other use of a third party API)?

- What are the estimated number of pages or screens for your app?

- Would you prefer to complete this app in a single pass or split it up into phases (each requiring separate budgets)?

- Have you already created the copy (text content)?

Time & money

- If you're working within a time frame or have been given a mandatory launch date, list it here. If the project will launch in phases, list proposed milestones and dates.

- Please tell us your budget for this project.

- Note: Sharing a realistic assessment of what you have to spend on this effort will help us scope the engagement appropriately. While disclosing your budget might not be something you typically do, sharing this information with us now will greatly reduce the likelihood of both sides spending significant time and resources "shooting in the dark."

Privacy

- Will we be required to sign a non-disclosure agreement (NDA) during the initial planning and negotiation phases?

- When this project is complete will we be able to share it, and our role in the project, publicly?

- It is our policy to turn over all final files and transfer of copyright on all projects. All unused ideas and design drafts remain our property.

WHERE TO LOOK FOR A FIRM

How can you find reliable, creative people?

Referrals: The best place to find your app team is by referral—ask your agency (if you have one) or ask your friends and colleagues. A personal recommendation is best for everyone. Don't forget to check LinkedIn for this if no one comes to mind.

Google: You can also find a good firm by Googling something like "mobile apps Utah" or wherever you live. While it's possible and totally fine to work with people out of state, it's nice if you can find people to meet with face-to-face. This can be especially good for apps because there is a lot of quick sketches and acting-out of concepts that is hard to do remotely.

Agencies: Look for agencies in your area and see who is doing apps by looking at their websites.

App sites: There are some great sites for finding teams such as GroupTalent or Elance (although I'd stay away from Elance, personally: You will be deluged with offshore freelancers).

Post an ad: You can post on Craigslist or on Twitter—just remember you'll get a wider response and range of candidates than if you hand pick them.

WHAT TO EXPECT WHEN YOU ARE PITCHED

Once you've narrowed down your short list of firms or individuals, you can start meeting with people and discussing the project. Take your time with these and notice that often it's more about the questions the firm asks during a conversation that tells you what they are like than what you see in their shiny portfolios.

A firm that is pitching you and sending a proposal should show their portfolio (or you should have seen it already, online or in person). The work and style should be something you like. If you are more drawn to clean lines and minimalism and all you see is heavily filtered dark stuff, they may not be right for you.

If the firm decides to submit a proposal it should outline what exactly will be delivered, the price, and a time estimate. Plan on seeing a series of change orders if the project deviates from the original statement of work — but as long as these are clearly explained and approved there won't be any nasty surprises.

Sometimes if you have a very large app a firm may want to do a discovery phase. In this phase you pay them a set amount to work with you to come up with a Statement of Work (SOW) and final proposal. If this makes you nervous, make sure that at the end of the discovery phase the Statement of Work document is your property and you can choose to continue with this firm or choose a different one and leverage the SOW for bids.

PLEASE NO RFPS

It may be tempting to just put all your information in a Request for Proposal (RFP), blast it out, and then compare answers and pricing. Please don't unless you want some of the best people to completely ignore your request.

RFPs are expensive and time consuming for firms to return. Often the people responding will not be the people you would ultimately work with. You are missing the opportunity to have conversations that show you the true personality and ability of the people you will end up spending this project time with. You will be left with a set of numbers and responses that are difficult to compare or get a final impression from.

You can still get three bids—you can even ask that the bids are similar in format because that is how your purchasing department requires it—but don't rob yourself of the best attention and talent you could have.

HOW TO CHOOSE FROM THE BIDS YOU RECEIVE

Ok, you have bids in hand and three strong candidates. You are probably not comparing apples to apples. You have an apple, an orange, and a pomegranate. You liked all three people, but how do you choose?

1) Is anyone's bid out of the ordinary?

- Is it really high? Is this because they are a large firm and you are paying for overhead, or are they the most experienced firm and actually know what they are getting into?

- Is it really low? So incredibly low? Are they either lying to get the business and will nickel and dime you later once you are too far into the project to back out, or do they not know enough to bid this properly?

2) Were there any nagging red flags?

- Was something just not right about the portfolio or the work they say they've done?

- Do they complain about past clients or give you the impression that you shouldn't check references with someone?

3) Will you be working with the person that pitched you?

- Or was that the sales person and you'll work through an account manager?

- If it was the designer/developer, do they have the business skills to take care of that side of the project?

4) What did you think of the portfolio?

- Was the work of consistent quality? Did they show a large enough body of work that you can make an accurate judgement?

Right now, as much as you are considering the numbers and the quantitative elements—you also have to listen to your head and your heart to pick the right person. The right partner makes unforeseen issues become something to work through together. The wrong partner makes unforeseen issues become $10,000 mistakes.

WHAT AN APP BUILD PROCESS LOOKS LIKE

Every agency is different and will go about things in a slightly different way, but every story still has a beginning, a middle, and an end. So does an app build project.

After a firm is chosen for your app project, a process similar to the one listed on the next page will take place. There will most likely be several iterations in each step. This process can take anywhere from a few weeks to a few months.

THE APP BUILD PROCESS

Proposal signed & initial deposit paid

Use cases + wireframes + SOW

Designs presented & approved

Designs packaged for development

Development (usually one platform at a time)

Full working version for client to approve

App approved by client

App submitted to distribution networks

Final payment / App launched

CASE STUDIES /
LET'S LOOK AT SOME APPS!

BOART LONGYEAR

The best use of QR codes I've seen.

The Boart Longyear App (iOS: iPhone/iPad; available free in the App Store) was created to provide a way for sales people all over the world to have every single marketing catalog with them at all times (without lugging around a 75 pound backpack).

It features a backend where the client can manage brochures on the fly (they push to the app). Sales people and potential clients can download the app, choose which brochure(s) they would like to receive, and send an email with a link to download these brochures.

One of the most interesting features of the app is the QR code reader. Basically it allows you to scan a Boart Longyear QR code and then connects you to the product landing page online and any related brochures. That's all well and good, but this sings when it's at a tradeshow.

QR codes are placed next to giant drill rigs and other equipment. Sales people armed with iPhones and iPads can discuss the equipment with interested parties and then scan the code and immediately send off the proper brochure. All of this happens in real time without the need for prospects to cart home heavy catalogs.

From the client's point of view:

What did you learn (as a client) about building an app that surprised you?

"I approached the app with a 'the sky's the limit' mentality, fully expecting pushback and 'you can't do that.' But I was amazed at the flexibility, simplicity, and capabilities of apps. We were able to integrate everything we were doing with marketing—ads, social media, landing pages, brochures, catalogs, even tradeshows—all into one app. Our app has become a very useful and successful tool for both our sales team and customers. Updates and additions to our collateral are now instantly distributed and maintained all in one place."

What advice would you give a client that is building their first app?

"When approaching a new app, keep all of the wild ideas on your spec list. This pushes the developers to think outside of the box and may lead to new ideas they provide that you hadn't envisioned. However, be realistic in your expectations for the first edition of your app. The beauty of an app is that you can always add new bells and whistles in subsequent releases. This keeps the app evolving and users engaged."

What is important to find in the team that builds your app?

"When searching for an app development team, look for a good balance between geek and nerd—a team that is creative with a marketing mind-set, but also has the techy programming skills to implement your ideas. User experience is paramount with apps. You should find a team that understands your audience and can foresee users' behavior. App users are a persnickety group and they don't tolerate clunky UIs that slow down their fast-paced world."

—**Cody Dingus,** *Global Marketing Manager, Boart Longyear*

◄ **Bonus Easter Egg:** This app was released on the heels of the new iPad (with Retina display). Boart Longyear's MarCom department travels the world to get amazing product and environment shots. If you load the app you will see these huge images on the menu page. Click the Spinner logo to cycle through the images.

Physical to Digital
The app helps connect physical pieces at a tradeshow with related digital assets that can be emailed to prospective customers.

SMARTMOUTH COMMUNICATIONS

[Brain + Mouth = Impact]

The SmartMouth App (iOS: iPhone/iPad; available for $6.99 in the App Store) was created to provide a speech coach in your pocket.

It takes the best of SmartMouth Communications' methods and advice and distills it into an app that you can use the next time you have to give a speech or presentation or run an important meeting.

This app is a great example of learning and doing—there is enough information to help you get on solid ground, and then the tools you need to act. The writing is fresh and fun and well worth the read.

From the client's point of view:

What advice would you give a client that is building their first app?

"You've got to let go. If you have an app developer with any experience and savvy, as I did, you've got to let go and let them run with it. There was no way I could've envisioned all the potential for the presentation and functionalities of my app, and, if I tried, I would've stunted the process. I trusted and turned it over to my developers and got an end result that is beyond what I could've imagined!"

—**Beth Noymer Levine, Principal,** *SmartMouth Communications*

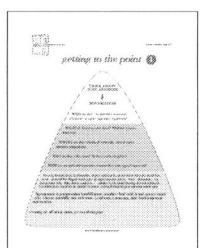
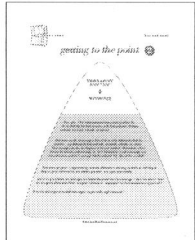
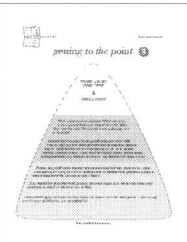
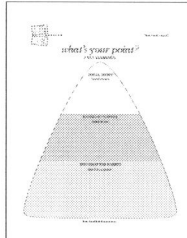
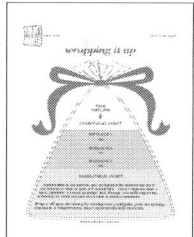

Transition from paper

The app was originally based on a series of paper handouts. It was updated to flow differently and add tools to work with the information.

THE MANDATE PRESS

"I want to be the first letterpress app out there."

The Letterpress Handbook App (iOS: iPhone; available for free in the App Store) was created to be a capsule experience around letterpress in general and The Mandate Press specifically.

The app was created to be a resource for designers and clients who like the look of letterpress but aren't quite sure about the ins and outs of modern letterpress printing. This app features a wealth of information organized into an FAQ, Glossary, Printing Tips, and Gallery. There was actually a point where I acted out what was supposed to happen with the navigation.

From the client's point of view:

What is important to find in the team that builds your app?

"Work with a firm that will work well with you. Even though you have hired someone to build this for you — you still have to do a lot to pull together your content. Choose people that are fun to work with and will help you get it done and not just leave it on you or shrug and say 'you didn't get back to me so I dropped the project off my work list'."

—**Ben Webster,** *Owner, The Mandate Press*

A not-too-subtle reminder.
To remind The Mandate Press that their FAQ content was due we delivered these giant mylar balloons.

TIMEMD

Beating competitors on price and features.

The TimeMD App (iOS: iPhone/iPad; Android Mobile/Android Tablet available for free in the App Store, Google Play, and Amazon Appstore for Android) is an access-point app created to allow employees to record time punches on the TimeMD system.

TimeMD was looking for a way to satisfy customers' requests for both a lower-priced timeclock and for a way to eliminate buddy punches (when one employee clocks in early or out late for another employee). They cooked up the idea to allow punches by taking an employee's picture—you put that on an iPad or a low priced Android device and you've got a great alternative.

Not only does the picture eliminate buddy punching, it tracks geolocation of time punches—ensuring that if you were supposed to be in Salt Lake City on a job, you actually were.

From the client's point of view:

What advice would you give a client that is building their first app?

"What surprised us most was that despite all our planning, within days of release, we immediately realized a few oversights in our application. This was a humbling reminder of one of the most significant differences between developing software applications vs. websites. With websites you have the liberty of making changes faster with far less overhead. Compared with software development, specifically for the iPad, you must respect the time and cost for posting even the most minor of changes."

— **Erik Rowland,** *Owner, TimeMD*

Visit www.buildingamobileapp.com/approval-from-the-trenches for more discussion of the challenges TimeMD faced with changes and approval.

A sketch to an app.
This app was kicked off with a crayon drawing on the table at a Mexican restaurant.

MORE /
REFERENCE & MORE HELP

ONLINE RESOURCES

I hope you found this book useful. I asked myself what I most wanted clients to know, looked over the blog posts I've written, did a lot of research, and applied what I've learned in the 10+ years I've been a designer—and what I've learned more recently designing and overseeing development of iOS, Android, and HTML5 apps.

RESOURCES

There are a lot of resources online to help with app building. Here are some of the best:

Teehan + Lax: This firm provides the absolute best Photoshop Files (PSDs) to use as start points for mobile apps. http://www.teehanlax.com/downloads/

iOS Human Interface Guidelines: This provides everything from best practices to creating files for building an iOS app. http://developer.apple.com/library/ios/#DOCUMENTATION/UserExperience/Conceptual/MobileHIG/Introduction/Introduction.html

Android User Interface Guidelines: This gives you everything to know about designing and developing for Android, from Android. http://developer.android.com/guide/practices/ui_guidelines/index.html

Can I Use...: This is a big list of what is available to use in HTML5: http://caniuse.com

STATISTICS

Distimo: app store data: http://www.distimo.com

ComScore: digital world statistics: http://www.comscore.com/

Flurry: analytics and lots of data. http://blog.flurry.com

Nielson: http://www.nielsen.com/us/en/insights.html

BLOGS

BGR: http://www.bgr.com/category/mobile-sections/

ArsTechnica: http://arstechnica.com/

Tech Crunch: http://techcrunch.com/mobile/

Mashable: http://mashable.com/tech/

EDUCATE YOURSELF TO TALK TO DESIGNERS AND DEVELOPERS

Hopefully you'll read everything in this book cover to cover. If so, this is more of a review session. If not, here is some high level stuff that will come up during an app proposal process that you'll want to understand.

GENERAL TERMS

» A **native app** is an app that is built to run on a specific platform only.

» **Platform** refers to all the pieces in a specific development chain—the company, the operating system, and the devices.

» An **HTML5 app** is the same thing as a **web app**—HTML is the language the web is written in and HTML5 refers to the latest code base that does app-type stuff.

» An **iOS app** runes on iPhone and iPad and is written with Objective-C.

» An **Android app** runs on Android devices and is written with Java.

» **Use cases** show the flow of a user through your app. These can include several different user personas, or just a general user. Use cases usually include all paths and deviations a user could take. See "Sample Use Case" on page 114.

» **Personas** are used in use cases to give an overall view of a type of user. A persona may have a name and will have attributes associated with it. For example, Cindy is a woman in her twenties who is just graduating from university and is looking for a job. Bob is man in his sixties who works at a large financial institution and is coming down the home stretch of his career path.

» **Wireframes** are usually black-and-white outlines of what could be on each page. They don't necessarily denote design, but help everyone account for all elements and functionality. See "Sample Wireframes" on page 115.

» **Gestures** are the different finger movements used to interact with an app. These are things like swipe, double tap, tap, and hold (see opposite page).

» A **Statement of Work (SOW)** is a document outlining each feature that will be built. These are incredibly boring and detailed, but this is where the rubber hits the road if there is any disagreement on what will be delivered.

» A **Change order** is a document that appends the original proposal or SOW to include new items, usually with an additional time and cost outline.

» **Work for hire** means that everything on the project is your property, including discarded design drafts and pieces of code. Normally projects will not be structured this way—the client will own the final product and copyright, but none of the discarded concepts or drafts.

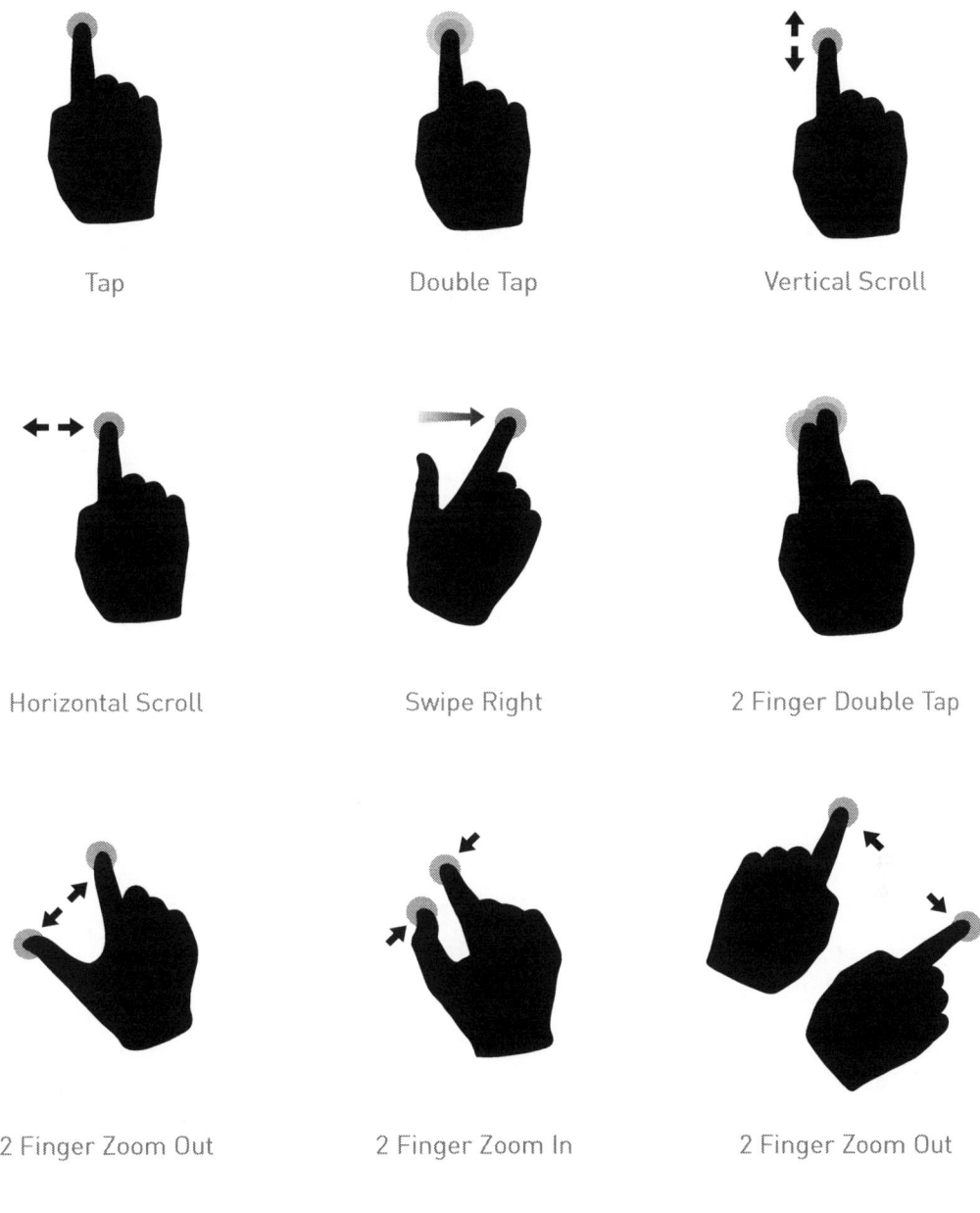

Different touch screen gestures that can be coded into an app.

DESIGN TERMS

» Designers use **Adobe Photoshop** (usually) to design apps. You will probably see JPGs or PNGs (flat graphics with no functionality) output from Photoshop to review design.

» **Fonts** are the different typefaces in an app. Apple comes with 56 prein-stalled, Android comes with 1 on Jelly Bean and 4 on older operating systems. More can be installed on either device. Fonts must be purchased and licensed.

» **Pixels** are the standard unit of measure in the digital world.

» **Icons** are little images used to connote an action or a label instead of text. Icon design is an art form in itself and many designers will purchase or find an open source icon set for a project instead of making these from scratch.

» **Stock photography** comes from stock websites and is found based on keywords. You pay a nominal fee and can license the work. You cannot use images you find on the web—they are all automatically copyrighted and illegal to use. You can find images from Flickr Advanced Search with Creative Commons licensing (free), or from microstock (cheap) sites like BigStock, iStockPhoto, or ShutterStock to use.

» **Resolution** is the size of a device, measured in pixels.

» **Density** is how many pixels per inch (PPI) the device has. More pixels crammed into a small space make things much crisper and less pixelated.

» **Responsive Design** is a term normally used for creating websites that have different user interfaces (UI) for each device (desktop, mobile, and tablet), but some of the same ideas apply to mobile/web apps.

» **User experience (UX)** is an area of study looking how the user interacts with a program and how they feel about it.

DEVELOPMENT TERMS

» Some **features** are easy to design and develop, some are difficult. It's always good to ask, but always weigh if the outcome is worth what it takes to build (return on investment [ROI] is more than just money, it's time and effort).

» **Local storage** refers to storing files and information on the device, instead of pushing it back to a central database. Information stored locally is only accessible on that device, while information in a database can be accessed from multiple devices.

» If information is stored in a **database** something has to connect the app in a person's hand with a database somewhere else in the world—this is usually an **application program interface (API)** and this is written to hook pieces of code together.

» Developers write **iOS apps** using the programing language **Objective-C** and use a program called **Xcode**.

» Developers write **Android apps** using the programing language **Java** and use a program called **Eclipse**.

» Developers write **HTML5 / web apps** using the language **HTML** and the markup **CSS** and may or may not use a specific program to do this.

Sample Use Case

Use cases are overview graphics that show the flow of an app. These can show different users, different events, and exception handling.

What the user **sees**

What the user **does**

STEP 1

App is installed

User sees app icon on device → User clicks app icon

STEP 2

QR Code

User sees a QR Code → User scans code with app

⚙ App **Accepts** code ⚙ App **Rejects** code

STEP 3

Display Relevant Information

Error Code with Option to Try Again

↓

Click Try Again (reload Step 2)

Sample Wireframes

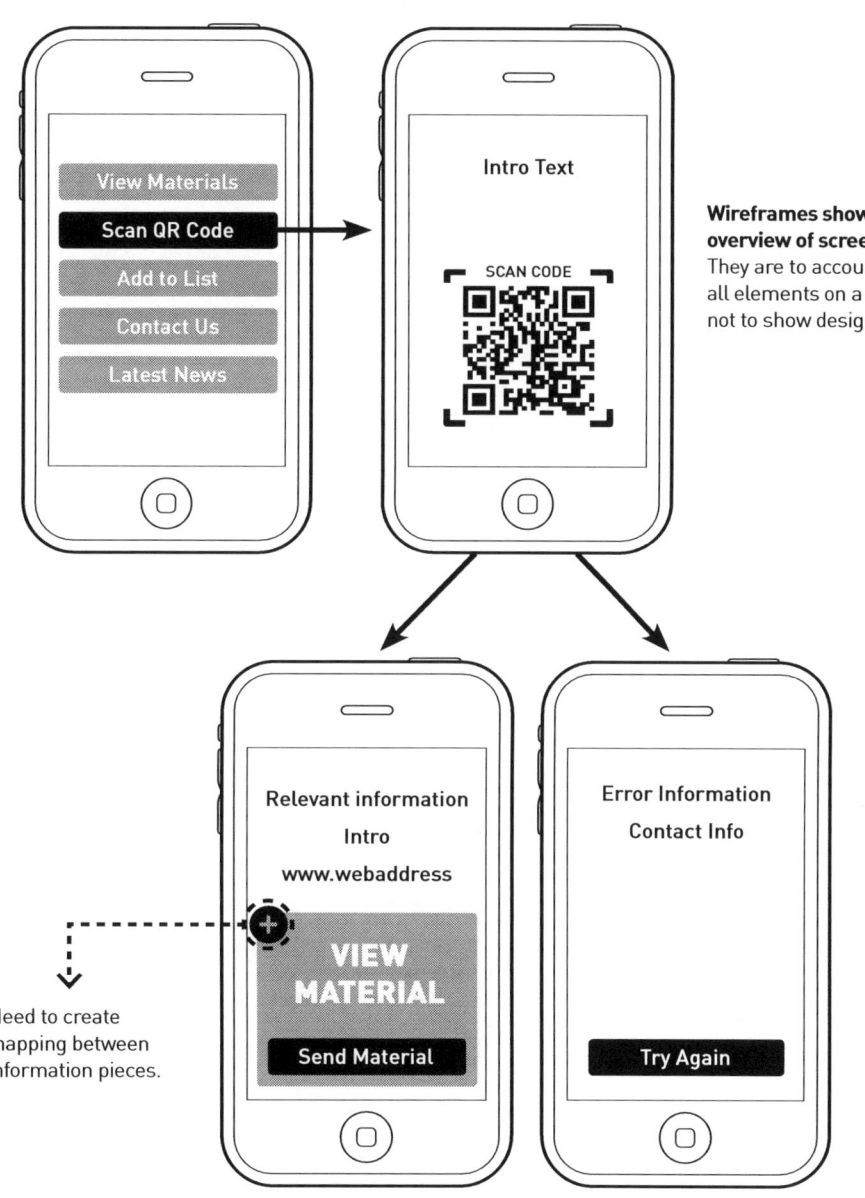

Wireframes show an overview of screens. They are to account for all elements on a page, not to show design.

Need to create mapping between information pieces.

10 MIN. /
EVERYTHING YOU NEED
TO KNOW IN THIS BOOK—
IN 10 MINUTES

EVERYTHING YOU NEED TO KNOW IN THIS BOOK—IN 10 MINUTES

TL;DR. Too long, didn't read. You skipped to the back to get the Cliff notes version, eh? Good for you—that's why I added this section. I have a really short attention span.

Just remember this is a briefing. To really understand this stuff you will want to look at the images, statistics, and charts throughout the book.

GET STARTED / GOOD THINGS TO KNOW

Who This Book is For

- Anyone who needs to build an app who isn't a designer or developer.

Proper Care and Feeding of Designers & Developers

- Be good to your designers and developers. Treat them as partners and keep them engaged.

Five Short Stories about Working with Designers & Developers

- **#1: Changes:** Anything regarding functionality needs to be discussed as early as possible. Arm yourself with knowledge of functional possibilities by downloading other well done apps and finding things you like. And frame your question as an *exploratory request*. Something like, "Is it possible at this point to change this from scrolling to a swipe? What would be involved in that?"

- **#2 : More Changes:** Sometimes it really is easy. Never be afraid to ask.

- **#3: Valid Feedback:** Feedback that comes from someone who isn't invested in the project or part of your target audience isn't necessarily valid. Design by committee creates watered down work.

- **#4: Trust Your Team:** Trust that your team has thought this through and is providing only the best solution to you.

- **#5: Client Responsibilities:** You are a partner in this project. From educating yourself on the project (thank goodness you bought this book!) to providing content in a timely fashion, you are as much a part of this project as the team you hire.

PART 1 / WHY BUILD A MOBILE APP

Why Build a Mobile App?

- Because you want to or have been told you have to.

- To create a Capsule Experience, Point of Access, Depth of Information, or Extended Capabilities (with a bunch of examples).

What Could Be a Good Mobile App for your Company?

- There is a quick list in this section.

Is There Money in Apps?

- Sure is.

Who Has a Mobile Device?

- Damn near everyone. 110 million people in the U.S., about 75 percent of the population.

- Tons of charts and stats in this section drilling into what people are doing on their devices, which platform they use, and some demographics. (Spoiler: old, rich, well educated people use iPhones and BlackBerrys).

"Why don't we just build a…"

- Reasons apps are better than websites/microsites/landing pages and PDFs/other electronic docs.

PART 2 / UNDERSTANDING APPS

Native vs. HTML5

- Native is an app the runs on a specific platform; HTML5 is a web app that runs in a browser on a device.

- 6 Big Questions to ask when choosing between native and HTML5.

Understanding Platforms

- Covers platforms, the development chain, and distribution.

Choosing a Platform

- Just go with iOS or Android and let people download them from the app stores.

- Don't touch Blackberry, there are too many buttons.

Resolution: A Tale of Pixels and Densities

- You only need to understand this if you are going to argue with your designer/developer about how an app looks on an iPhone versus a Galaxy Tab.

- Welcome to Android fragmentation.

Building an iOS App

- iOS apps are built in Objective-C and need a lot of different images.

- Apple receives 30 percent of everything—you can cry all you want, but thems the breaks.

- People upgrade their iOS versions quickly and regularly.

- Some info on designing and developing for iOS.

Building an Android App

- Android apps are built in Java and need even more images than an iPhone app but with far less understandable sizes. Seriously, who wrote that spec?

- People don't upgrade their operating system versions very quickly, partially because of carrier and device manufacturer meddling.

- Some info on designing and developing for Android.

Building an HTML5/Web App

- If you build an HTML5 app you will need to support IE 9+, Safari 5+, Chrome 16+ Firefrox 13+, Android (Jelly Bean, Ice Cream Sandwich, and Honeycomb), iOS 5+. Don't even think about Silk (Amazon's browser) or older versions of desktop browsers.

Pricing an App

- Go free or paid—but plan to make your money via in-app purchases.

PART 3 / GETTING YOUR APP BUILT

What Does an App Cost?

- Another spoiler alert—it costs a lot of money. There is a lot that goes into it. And yes, I share some numbers in this section.

How to Hire a Firm

- Know what you're looking for, but also find someone you really like. This isn't all about price, it's about working with someone that you enjoy working with and getting the right thing produced.

Worksheet: App Planning

- Exactly what it says on the tin! A worksheet to help put your app in motion and have a basis to talk to firms.

- Get some broad ideas of what you are asking for. The next person that says, "I have the best idea for an app but I don't know anything about them" gets punched.

Where to Look For A Firm

- Get a referral, look online, handpick when you can, or put out an ad.

What to Expect When You Are Pitched

- A portfolio, a proposal, and some pricing.

Please No RFPs

- Why they're a waste of everyone's time.

How to Choose from the Bids You Receive

- Pick someone you really like for lots of reasons.

What an App Build Process Looks Like

- A timeline-style graph with the basic milestones.

CASE STUDIES / LET'S LOOK AT SOME APPS!

- Specifically, let's look at some apps my firm produced for Boart Long-year, SmartMouth Communications, The Mandate Press, and TimeMD.

- Includes remarks from clients—things they want other people to know when they do an app project.

- Also includes screen shots and behind-the-scenes stories.

MORE / REFERENCE & MORE HELP

More Resources
- Lists of web resources, statistic houses, and blogs.

Educate Yourself to Talk to Designers and Developers
- A big list of notes (or a cleverly disguised glossary) to make friends and influence your app.

Sample Use Case & Wireframes
- A short, sweet, high level look at what these documents typically look like.

About the Author
- My name is Amber Sawaya.
  This is my first book and I appreciate you reading it.

- You can reach me at my:
  book site - www.buildingamobileapp.com
  author site - www.ambersawaya.com
  corporate site - www.sawayaconsulting.com

PLEASE LEAVE A REVIEW

If you enjoyed this book please consider leaving me a review on Amazon.

I read every review and have worked hard to create a book that will be a valuable resource for clients and corporations staring an app project.

I welcome comments and questions through my book website www.buildingamobileapp.com or through Facebook and Google+

ACKNOWLEDGMENTS

Thank you to my business and life partner Steve. Your support, talent, dev skills, and mad anti-gravity yoga moves are what have allowed us to create our awesome life together. Thank you to my best friend and partner-designer Kira for her inspiration, input, and hours of design work on this book. Thank you to my friend and editor Karen for helping me say what I want to say without looking a fool.

ABOUT THE AUTHOR

Amber Sawaya is a best-selling author, designer and business owner located in Salt Lake City, Utah. She is passionate about the business she and her partner own—and the way they do business.

This is her first book.

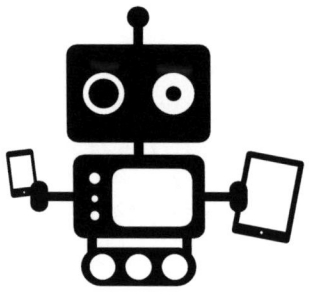

4020901R00081

Printed in Great Britain
by Amazon.co.uk, Ltd.,
Marston Gate.